LORRAINE PASCALE'S
Fast, Fresh and Easy Food

LORRAINE PASCALE'S
Fast, Fresh and Easy Food

100 Fabulous,
Easy to Make Recipes

Photographs by Myles New

HarperCollins*Publishers*

HarperCollins*Publishers*
77–85 Fulham Palace Road,
Hammersmith, London W6 8JB

www.harpercollins.co.uk

First published by HarperCollins*Publishers* 2012

10 9 8 7 6 5 4 3

Text © Lorraine Pascale, 2012

Photographs © Myles New, 2012

Lorraine Pascale asserts her moral right to be identified
as the author of this work

A catalogue record of this book is available from the
British Library

ISBN 978-0-00-748966-4

Food styling: Katie Giovanni and Julia Azzarello
Props styling: Lisa Harrison

Printed and bound in the UK by
Butler Tanner & Dennis Ltd, Frome, Somerset

Devised and presented by Lorraine Pascale and produced
by BBC Bristol.

MIX
Paper from
responsible sources
FSC C007454

FSC™ is a non-profit international organisation established to promote the
responsible management of the world's forests. Products carrying the FSC
label are independently certified to assure consumers that they come from
forests that are managed to meet the social, economic and ecological needs
of present and future generations, and other controlled sources.

Find out more about HarperCollins and the environment at
www.harpercollins.co.uk/green

Contents

Introduction

Staring at the blank page with my deadline looming, no words seemed to be coming. A relaxed, unpressurised atmosphere is usually when a flurry of inspiration hits, but it wasn't until I was on a plane ride back from sunny, siliconed Los Angeles with a glass of Californian Chardonnay on my tiny table that the words began to flow.

I thought back to my first book, *Baking Made Easy*, a self-explanatory title packed with recipes that, in my own words, covered 'anything cooked in the oven'. The broad definition allowed me artistic licence to develop meals and dishes both sweet and savoury. Exotic tarts and traditional cakes featured alongside night-time nibbles and Parisian patisserie. With my next book and series, *Home Cooking Made Easy*, came food with a more homely note: comforting casseroles and lasagnes, beauteous breads and simple puddings and desserts.

It felt, for the meantime anyway, that I'd had a significant part of my cooking repertoire covered and that this time I wanted to try something a little bit different, something that would hopefully prove even more useful for the (sadly) ever-decreasing time in which we have to prepare and cook food. I don't know how often I have come home from a day whizzing around like the Energizer Bunny on the rampage to a family awaiting some culinary delight. I also don't know how many times I have hung my head in shame and uttered the words, 'Oh. Yes. Dinner,' and then made the short trip to the local supermarket to try to buy from the near-empty shelves and then cobble something together for dinner.

I am not at all embarrassed to say that on many occasions I have returned home to the waiting party laden with food that just needs a simple peeling back of the plastic and a slight turn of the oven dial, usually to 180°C. These ready-meals serve a purpose and I am thankful that they exist, but I wondered what if a book existed that was jam-packed full of dishes that were quick, simple, nutritious and above all super-tasty? I wrote this book for the many, many people out there who, like me and my family, face the same daily dilemma of 'What on earth is for dinner?'

Thanks to the brilliant medium of Twitter, countless readers have told me that the important thing for the evening meal is that it is easy and quick to cook, using ingredients that don't require a space shuttle flight to the outer reaches of the solar system to source. The main ingredients people seem to favour are chicken (breasts, not so much the thigh or the leg), lamb chops, pork chops, minced beef or lamb, and fish. So I've included an enormous range of dishes featuring these, along with other tasty fare such as duck and vegetarian grub. I don't know if it is the Brit in me, but with my meal I like to eat some kind of a veg and/or a carb, but not any ordinary side dish — something a bit different that will leave (even with the quickest of meals) a lasting sensory memory on my tongue and in my mind.

Dishes such as the Italian Cacciatore get a gentle lift with the help of the mildly spiced harissa, a red chilli paste from North Africa. A simple Salmon en Croute is transformed by the use of papery filo in which to envelop it, and the accompanying potatoes are gently crushed with a pesto made from basil and curly kale. A Lamb Biryani, cooked in one pot and ready to eat in 25 minutes, is delicately spiced with the very-easy-to-find garam masala, cumin and chilli powder.

My current favourite are Lemoncello Jello Shots — lemon wedges scraped clean of their flesh and filled with a citrusy alcoholic (or not, if you so choose) jelly — that are so simple to make and yet so attention-getting when served, and of course super-yumbelicious to eat.

The goal of this book was to create something people would revisit time and time again. A cookbook that would be on that kitchen counter several times a week, for busy people who love good food and want to make something quick and easy, with tasty and accessible ingredients, to impress family and friends. And I wanted to provide an entire meal: main dish and side. So often when you know what you want to cook, it is challenging to figure out what to have with it. With this book, I have served up dishes with an accompaniment or two, making mealtimes much easier to plan. I also tried to make it as simple as possible so that everything is served up together, with a time plan for each recipe so you can sail through the instructions and end up with a delicious dish in super-fast time. I have put my heart and soul into this book and hope it helps you to serve up fast, fresh and delicious meals every day.

Lorraine

A few handy tips on the recipes

+ All preparation and cooking times are an estimate so check and taste things as they cook.

+ Always wash rice thoroughly before use.

+ I find it best to have all the ingredients and equipment out ready before you start cooking, so everything is easy to get when you need it.

+ These recipes have all been tested a minimum of four times, and they have been written so that everything is ready at the same time. So if you follow the method to the letter you will have quick and tasty meals ready in flash.

+ Some recipes have a start to finish time so you know roughly how long it will take from the moment you start cooking to when you finish.

+ Other recipes are split between preparation time and cooking/baking time. So the prep time is the hands on time and the rest of the time whilst the dish is in the oven is free time!

+ Some recipes are super-fast and others have an element to them which is faster than the usual way of prepping or cooking the dish.

+ The equipment list is not exhaustive but a guide to the main pieces of kitchen equipment you will need to prepare the dish. Everyday smaller utensils required are not included in the list.

+ If you have any cooking questions, please do Tweet me @lorrainepascale. I receive lots of Tweets and cannot guarantee to answer to every one, but I will do my best!

Canapés + cocktails

'Be kind, for everyone you meet is fighting a hard battle.'
Plato

I would love to profess that friends drop by
unexpectedly, so I have to rustle something up quickly
for an impromptu feast, but the reality is that never
really happens. What does tend to happen is that,
in true Lorraine Pascale style, I am always rushing
around, slightly disorganised and with the clock ticking
away, having known for weeks that some people
are coming round and always leaving it to the very
last minute to get everything together! These simple
canapés (and of course cocktails) are the perfect
solution to this modern-day madness of rush, rush,
rush. So easy to prepare and super-tasty too,
with that ever-important 'wow' factor on the plate.

Time from start to finish:
20 minutes
Makes: 24
Equipment: Large baking sheet,
3 small bowls

Crostini bases

1 French baguette
Extra virgin olive oil
1 garlic clove

Tomato, basil & mint

2 large ripe tomatoes
Extra virgin olive oil
Small handful of fresh basil and
mint leaves
Pinch of sugar (optional)

White bean, prosciutto & rocket

100g tinned cannellini beans
2 slices of prosciutto
Small handful of wild rocket

Goat's cheese, figs & mint with balsamic drizzle

100g soft goat's cheese
2 fresh figs
Small handful of small fresh mint leaves
Drizzle of balsamic vinegar
1 squidge of honey
Salt and freshly ground black pepper

Quick-cook canapé crostini

These really easy canapés have saved the day, not only when (in the very rare event) people drop by my house unannounced, but also when I fancy a quick snack of an evening. It is great to get creative with these: see what is in your cupboard and fridge, throw some ingredients together and experiment! I have used the oven to crisp up the crostini, but they can be put in the toaster or under the grill to get the same effect. If you crisp them up first, they won't need as much time to cook.

+ Preheat the oven to 190°C, (fan 170°C), 375°F, Gas Mark 5.

+ Trim the ends off the baguette and cut it into 24 diagonal slices, about 2cm thick. Place on a large baking sheet, drizzle with oil and bake for 7–8 minutes.

+ In the meantime, prepare the toppings.

+ For the tomato one, roughly chop the tomatoes and place in a small bowl. Drizzle a little oil over, rip up the basil and mint leaves and add them along with salt, pepper and sugar to taste. Toss everything together.

+ Then, for the white bean topping, put the cannellini beans in a small bowl, add a good drizzle of oil, season with salt and pepper and then mash roughly with a fork. Cut the slices of prosciutto in half.

+ Finally, for the goat's cheese crostini, mash the goat's cheese with a fork in a small bowl and season, then cut the figs into eighths.

+ Remove the crostini from the oven. They should be just crisp. Cut the garlic clove in half and rub the cut edge all over their tops.

+ Now, to assemble, simply spoon the tomato mixture onto eight of the crostini. Arrange the rocket on eight more, dollop the crushed beans on top, then lightly scrunch up the prosciutto and arrange on top of each one. Finally, spread the goat's cheese over the remaining eight crostini, arrange a couple of pieces of fig on top of each, scatter the mint leaves over and drizzle with a little balsamic and honey.

+ Arrange the crostini on a large serving platter or cake stand and serve.

Time from start to finish:
25 minutes
Serves: 4
Equipment: Baking tray, 2 wide,
shallow bowls, small bowl

Vegetable oil (or spray oil)

2 medium eggs

100g dried natural breadcrumbs (or polenta)

1 tsp English mustard powder

2 stalks of fresh flat leaf parsley or thyme (optional)

4 medium skinless, boneless chicken breasts

Honey mustard dip

100ml mayonnaise

3 tbsp wholegrain mustard

2 squidges of honey

2 limes

Salt and freshly ground black pepper

Crispy, crunchy chicken strips with honey mustard dip

Being a tactile person at heart, eating food with my fingers is pure luxury for me. I have a favourite surf-and-turf restaurant I frequent with the family and I regularly order their crispy chicken tenders for a starter. The piquant honey mustard dip has me getting right on in there with a spoon and eating up every last morsel.

+ Preheat the oven to 200°C, (fan 180°C), 400°F, Gas Mark 6. Lightly grease a baking tray with oil and set aside. I like to do this quickly with a spray oil.

+ Crack the eggs into a wide, shallow bowl and beat lightly to bring together. Tip the breadcrumbs (or polenta) and mustard powder into another wide, shallow bowl. Pick the leaves from the parsley or thyme then finely chop them before tossing through the breadcrumbs with some salt and pepper.

+ Cut each chicken breast lengthways into three strips. Dip each piece into the egg, shaking off the excess, and then into the breadcrumbs to coat evenly. Arrange on the baking tray as you go. I tend to get in a sticky mess with this as the egg on my hands becomes coated with breadcrumbs, but the end result is so worth it.

+ Bake in the oven for around 12 minutes, turning each piece of chicken over halfway through.

+ Meanwhile, to make the dip, put the mayonnaise into a small bowl with the wholegrain mustard and honey and stir to combine. Season to taste with salt and pepper.

+ Cut the limes into quarters and add the juice of one piece to the dip, squeeze by squeeze, tasting as you go until you are happy. The lime lifts the dip's flavours a little and gives a nice balance. Spoon the dip into a small serving bowl and place in the centre of a large plate.

+ Remove the chicken from the oven. When cooked, it should be piping hot in the centre and crispy and golden brown on the outside.

+ Arrange the chicken around the dip on the plate and serve with the remaining lime wedges.

Pancetta & Parmesan puffs

Prep time: 25 minutes
Time baking in the oven:
25 minutes
Makes: about 25
Equipment: 2 baking sheets,
small frying pan, medium
pan, grater, 2 medium bowls,
disposable piping bag (optional)

50g butter
125ml milk
50g pancetta cubes
Oil
25g Parmesan cheese
75g plain flour
1 tsp chilli powder (optional)
Pinch of salt
2 medium eggs

I know, I have done it again. Pancetta. It's that porky, tasty yumminess that I love so very much. Now these cheesy little numbers are made from choux pastry, which for me is the easiest pastry on the block. A positive word of warning: these are incredibly moreish. A just-cooked bowl of them will disappear in literally minutes.

+ Preheat the oven to 170°C, (fan 150°C), 325°F, Gas Mark 3. Line two baking sheets with baking parchment and set aside.

+ Put a small frying pan on a medium heat for the pancetta.

+ Put the butter and milk in a medium pan over a low heat and leave the butter to melt.

+ Meanwhile, place the pancetta into the frying pan with a drizzle of oil and cook for about 4 minutes, turning every so often.

+ Once the butter has melted into the milk, whack up the heat and bring to the boil.

+ Meanwhile, finely grate the Parmesan and tip it into a medium bowl. Stir in the flour, chilli powder, if you like, and a pinch of salt.

+ As soon as the buttery milk boils, remove the pan from the heat and add the flour mixture to it. Beat it really hard with a wooden spoon until the mixture starts to leave the sides of the pan. Then tip it into a medium bowl, spread it out all around the inside and leave it for a few minutes until cool to the touch.

+ Once the pancetta is crisp and golden, remove from the heat and tip onto kitchen paper to drain off excess fat and set aside.

+ Once the flour mix has cooled down a little, add the eggs, one at a time, beating hard between each addition. When the egg first goes in, the mixture will look a little less than pleasant, as if it won't mix in, but keep beating it really hard and it will come good. Then stir in the pancetta.

+ Now, here you can either spoon blobs of the choux pastry onto the baking sheets or (my favourite method with my piping bag obsession)

>

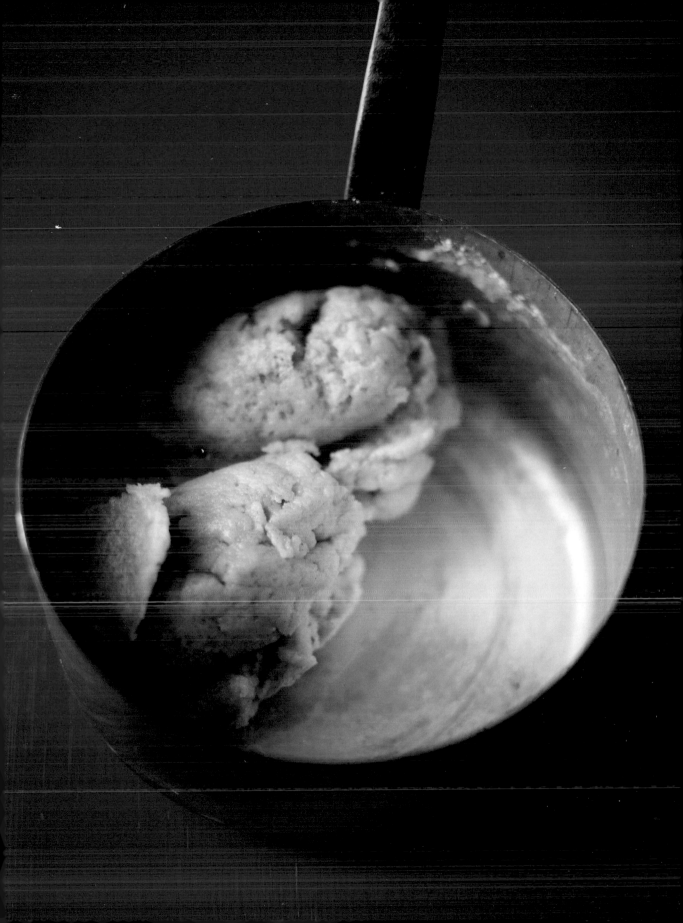

Pancetta &
Parmesan puffs

(continued)

pipe the blobs using a disposable piping bag cut to give a 1.5cm opening. Either way, make them about 2–3cm in diameter and space them a little bit apart. This makes about 25. Use a finger slightly moistened with water to push down any end bits that may be sticking up (so they don't burn in the oven), then bake for 25 minutes.

+ The puffs should be crisp and golden on top when cooked. These are really best served piping hot when they are still slightly moist as they are cut open.

Time from start to finish:
15 minutes
Serves: 4
Equipment: Colander, blender
or food processor, large frying
pan, plate

Hummus

400g tin of chickpeas

I garlic clove

100g half- or full-fat crème fraîche

1–4 tbsp harissa paste (easy to find at
the supermarket)

Drizzle of extra virgin olive oil
(optional)

Halloumi

Sunflower oil

50g plain flour

2 x 250g blocks of halloumi cheese

1 lime

Small handful of fresh coriander

Salt and freshly ground black pepper

Crunchy black pepper halloumi dip sticks with harissa hummus

Before I tested this recipe I had not had the privilege of cooking halloumi. I'd eaten it many times, but never felt the urge to give it a go at home. Halloumi is an eccentric-textured-and-tasting cheese which is very salty on the palate. It prefers, unlike its cheesy counterparts, to be pan-fried and grilled as it holds itself together very well once cooked.

+ First, make the hummus. Drain and rinse the chickpeas, peel the garlic and add both to a blender or food processor. Add the crème fraîche and enough harissa paste to taste (depending on how hot you like it). Blitz until smooth, season to taste with salt and pepper and add a drizzle of oil if you think it needs it. Then spoon it into a serving bowl and set aside.

+ Next, prepare the halloumi. Put three big glugs of oil in a large frying pan over a medium heat. Put the flour on a plate, season with a little pepper and set aside. Cut the halloumi into thick sticks. I cut each block into quarters lengthways and then lay each piece on its side and cut it in half again to give eight big chunky chips. Toss them in the flour so they are well covered, then gently lower them into the hot oil and fry for 4–5 minutes, turning regularly with tongs, until golden brown all over.

+ Remove the halloumi from the pan and drain on kitchen paper for a minute. Then arrange on a large serving plate and squeeze the lime juice over. Sit the dip bowl on the plate beside the halloumi, pick and scatter the coriander leaves on top and serve. Halloumi really comes to life with these flavours.

Time from start to finish:
25 minutes
Serves: 6
Equipment: Colander, 2 small
bowls, 25.5cm-square baking
dish at least 6cm deep

Salsa

200g jar red or green jalapeños

200g cherry tomatoes

1 red onion (or 1 bunch of spring onions)

Small handful of fresh coriander

Nachos

200g Cheddar cheese

400g tin of kidney beans

200g bag of tortilla chips

200g sour cream

Guacamole

3 perfectly ripe avocados

A few drops of Tabasco sauce (optional)

½ lime

Salt and freshly ground black pepper

Naughty, naughty nachos

Lots of cheese, chips and cream. Just what I feel I need on those days when I want that extra bit of comfort on a plate. There are a few parts to this recipe, but it is really, really quick and I find myself gravitating to make this at the weekend, as it is a great sharing dish. It is on the side of naughty, but really tasty. Everything in balance is my mantra. I found the jars of jalapeños in the supermarket, but if you can't get them, just use two regular green or red chillies, deseeded and finely sliced.

+ Preheat the oven to 200°C, (fan 180°C), 400°F, Gas Mark 6.

+ Firstly, prepare the salsa. Drain the jalapeños, quarter the cherry tomatoes and toss both into a small bowl. Peel and finely chop the red onion (or finely slice the spring onions, if using), reserve a small handful and add the remainder to the bowl. Rip the leaves from the coriander stalks, roughly chop them, then toss everything together and season to taste.

+ Finely grate the cheese and drain and rinse the beans.

+ Now to assemble the nachos. Scatter a third of the tortilla chips in the bottom of the baking dish and scatter over a third of the cheese and then all of the beans. Then follow with a third more tortillas, a third more cheese and some of the salsa. Finish with the remaining tortillas and cheese. This is actually a total freeform dish; my only thing is I love cheese on the top.

+ Now pop it into the oven to bake for 10 minutes while you make the guacamole.

+ Halve the avocados, discard the stones and use a spoon to scoop the flesh out into a small bowl. Lightly mash with a fork and then stir the reserved chopped onion through with a few drops of Tabasco, if you like. Season to taste with salt and pepper and squeeze in the lime juice.

+ Spoon the sour cream, remaining tomato salsa and guacamole into small serving bowls. Remove the now-cooked nachos from the oven. The cheese should be bubbling and the tortillas just catching colour. Serve in the centre of the table with the accompaniments for everyone to dig in and help themselves.

Time from start to finish (for
all three): **15 minutes** (about
5 minutes each)
Equipment: **2 medium bowls,
scissors, colander, blender**

Skinny dipping

Three tasty, no-cook skinny dip numbers; great to eat with potato-skin crisps, tortilla chips or crudités such as carrots, radishes and celery. You can make them all or just one or two. They can all be made ahead of time for stress-free snacking!

Tuna & crème fraîche dip with black pepper
Makes: **about 225g**

185g or 200g tin of tuna in spring water
75g half- or full-fat crème fraîche
A few fresh chives
¼ lime (or lemon)
Teeny squidge of honey (optional)
Salt and freshly ground black pepper

Tuna & créme fraîche dip with black pepper
+ Drain the tuna well, squeezing out as much of the water as possible. Place in a medium bowl, add the crème fraîche and then snip in the chives using scissors. Mix together well and season to taste with salt, pepper and a good squeeze of lime (or lemon) juice. Add a little honey to sweeten, if liked, also. Spoon into a serving bowl to serve.

Hummus with cumin & paprika
Makes: **about 350g**

400g tin of chickpeas
100g half- or full-fat crème fraîche
2 tsp cumin powder
Extra virgin olive oil
1 garlic clove
¼ lime (or lemon)
A good pinch of paprika
A few fresh coriander or flat leaf parsley leaves
Salt and freshly ground black pepper

Hummus with cumin & paprika
+ Drain the chickpeas, rinse well and then tip them into a blender (I find a stick blender brilliant). Add the crème fraîche, cumin and a drizzle of oil, then peel and add the garlic clove. Season well with salt and pepper and blitz until fairly smooth. Check the seasoning, adjusting if necessary, add a squeeze of lime (or lemon) juice and then blitz again briefly. Spoon into a serving bowl, sprinkle the paprika on top, rip over some coriander or parsley leaves and serve.

Avocado, chilli & chive dip
Makes: **about 275g**

2 ripe avocados
1 small red chilli
A few fresh chives
1 lime (or lemon)
Salt and freshly ground black pepper

Avacado, chilli & chive dip
+ Cut the avocados in half, discard the stones and then scoop out the flesh into a medium bowl. Deseed and finely slice the chilli and add. Then, using scissors, snip in the chives. Mash everything up until fairly smooth, season to taste with a good amount of salt and pepper and squeeze in the lime (or lemon) juice. Spoon into a serving bowl to serve.

Prep time: 15 minutes
Setting time: 30 minutes in the freezer (or 1 hour in the fridge)
Makes: 20–28 (depending on the size of lemons used)
Equipment: Kettle, small wide bowl, large tray or 12-hole muffin tin, heatproof measuring jug

Seven 6.5 x 11.5cm or eight 7.5 x 11cm leaves of gelatine

7 medium or 5 big lemons

135g pack of lemon jelly

400ml hot water

Couple of small drops of lemon essence (optional)

1 tbsp caster sugar

Lemoncello jello shots

Remove these sassy sunshine slices from the freezer or fridge an hour or so before you want to use them so they soften slightly before eating. Of course, these can be made for the kiddies, but for adults I like to add 150ml of lovely, luscious limoncello (see p35) to 350ml of water. No need to heat it; just dissolve the jelly in boiling water, add the gelatine leaves, then finish with the limoncello and sugar.

+ Put the kettle on to boil. Then put the gelatine leaves into a small wide bowl, cover them with cold water and set aside to soften.

+ Cut the lemons in half lengthways and, using a spoon, scoop out the juicy flesh. It takes a bit of wiggling and getting squirted by the juice, but you will get there! The trick is not to break through the skin. (You don't need the flesh here, but afterwards I like to squeeze the juice out and freeze it in an ice-cube tray for handy lemon juice needs at other times.)

+ Set each lemon shell half, cut side up, on a large tray or put each one in the hole of a 12-hole muffin tin. If you have 14 shells, then nestle the remaining two on top in between the others and they should sit still.

+ Next, break up the lemon jelly a bit and put it into a heatproof measuring jug, then pour over enough hot water to reach 400ml in the jug.

+ Pick up the gelatine leaves – they will feel all soft. Gently squeeze out as much liquid as you can from them, discard the bowl of water and then put the soft gelatine leaves into the jelly and hot water. Stir constantly until it dissolves. Then stir in the lemon essence (sometimes the lemon jelly just is not lemony enough) and sugar until dissolved.

+ Use the jelly to fill each lemon shell right up to the very top so it is almost overflowing. Let them cool down for about 5 minutes and then whack them in the freezer for 30 minutes to firm up (but not much longer or they will freeze!). They will set in the fridge also, but allow double the time.

+ Once they are firm, remove them from the freezer (or fridge). Then, using a sharp, non-serrated knife, cut them in half, straight down, lengthways, and there you have it!

Prep time: 25 minutes
Setting time: 25 minutes in the
freezer, plus 15 minutes if using
passion fruit seeds
Makes: 56–64 (depending on the
size of limes used)
Equipment: Kettle, small wide
bowl, large tray or 2–3 x
12-hole muffin tins, heatproof
measuring jug

Seven 6.5 x 11.5cm or eight 7.5 x
11cm leaves of gelatine

16 small or 14 medium limes

135g pack of strawberry jelly

400ml hot water

1 tbsp caster sugar (optional)

1 large or 2 small passion fruit
(optional)

Watermelon jello shots

If you were a sporty type at school, you may remember those little orange slices that were given out at half-time during matches. A momentary respite from jumping and leaping in the air on a cold windy netball court in the depths of winter seems to be a vivid memory from my early teenage years. Naturally, giving you a recipe for orange slices may have proven uninspiring so, with a bit of cooking magic, I would like to introduce you to my watermelon jello shots … A happy walk down memory lane with a very modern twist. For an alcoholic version, replace 150ml of the water with some vodka.

+ Put the kettle on to boil. Then put the gelatine leaves into a small wide bowl, cover them with cold water and set aside to soften.

+ Cut the limes in half lengthways, rather than around their middles and, using a spoon, scoop out the juicy flesh. It takes a bit of wiggling and getting squirted by the juice, but you will get there! The trick is not to break through the lime skin. (You don't need the flesh for this recipe, but afterwards I like to squeeze the juice out and freeze it in an ice-cube tray for handy lime juice needs at other times.)

+ Set each half, cut side up, on a large tray, or put each one in the hole of a 12-hole muffin tin. They fit perfectly and don't move around too much that way. You will need two or three 12-hole muffin tins, but if you don't have enough, you can nestle the excess lime shells on top in between the others and they should sit still.

+ Next, break up the strawberry jelly a bit and put it into a heatproof measuring jug and then pour enough hot water over the jelly to reach 400ml in the jug.

+ Pick up the gelatine leaves – they will feel all soft. Gently squeeze out as much liquid as you can from them, discard the bowl of water and then put the soft gelatine leaves into the jelly and hot water. Leave to stand for a few minutes until everything begins to melt, then stir a little until

>

Watermelon jello shots

(continued)

everything is completely dissolved. Next, stir in the sugar, if using, until dissolved also.

+ Use the jelly to fill each lime shell right up to the very top so it is almost overflowing. Let them cool down for about 5 minutes and then whack them in the freezer for about 25 minutes to firm up (but not much longer or they will freeze!). They will set in the fridge also, but allow double the time.

+ Meanwhile, prepare the passion fruit by cutting it (or them) in half and scooping out the seeds onto kitchen paper. Dab the seeds dry with the paper and set them aside.

+ Halfway through the setting time (once the jellies are just beginning to firm up), remove them and carefully arrange the passion fruit seeds on top. Arrange about six seeds on each one, keeping them away from the middle as you will be cutting them in half later, and lightly press each one down a little so it will set into the jelly. Then return to the freezer until completely firm.

+ Once they are firm, remove them from the freezer. Then, using a sharp, non-serrated knife, cut them in half, straight down (again, lengthways), and there you have it!

Time from start to finish:
15 minutes
Makes: 4
Equipment: Four 350ml glasses,
rolling pin, straws or cocktail
stirrers

3 limes

8 tbsp demerara sugar

12 strawberries

400g crushed ice

Small handful of fresh mint

250ml white rum

250ml soda water or lemonade
(or even Pimm's)

Strawberry & mint mojitos

Ahh, mojitos. My Achilles heel, for sure. Whether they be alcoholic or virgin, I love these sugary South American drinks. Strawberries can be substituted with other fruit, such as blackberries or raspberries, and the rum replaced with extra soda water or lemonade for a non-alcoholic version.

+ Cut the limes into quarters lengthways and put three pieces in the bottom of each of four 350ml serving glasses. Make sure the glasses are wide enough to fit the end of a rolling pin in. (You'll see why.)

+ Add 2 tablespoons of the sugar to each one. Then, using the end of a rolling pin, squash everything together to squeeze the lime juice out and mix with the sugar.

+ Hull the strawberries (cut out the green bit with the point of a sharp knife) and add three to each glass. Then very gently crush them a bit too.

+ Fill the glasses almost to the top with the crushed ice. Pick and reserve four nice mint sprigs from the bunch and then rip the remaining leaves off the stalks and scatter them onto the ice. Divide the rum evenly between the glasses and then top with the soda water or lemonade.

+ Mix everything together with a spoon, then add a sprig of mint to each glass and serve at once with a straw or cocktail stirrer popped in.

Prep time: 10 minutes
Infusing time: from 1 day to
3 months
Makes: 1 litre
Equipment: Medium pan, zester,
1-litre glass bottle with a stopper
or a Kilner jar (sterilised – see
right), fine sieve

300g granulated sugar
200ml cold water
8 lemons
600ml vodka

Lovely limoncello

To prepare the containers for this luscious lemon drink, sterilise a 1-litre glass bottle with a stopper or a Kilner jar in the dishwasher on the hottest wash, or carefully put them in just-boiled water (off the heat) for a couple of minutes and dry with a clean tea towel.

+ Put the sugar in a medium pan over a low to medium heat with the water. Cook for a few minutes, giving it a stir from time to time, until the sugar has melted. Then turn up the heat, bring to the boil and leave to bubble away for 2 minutes.

+ Meanwhile, give the lemons a wash in hot soapy water to get rid of the shiny, waxy coating and then rinse and dry them well. Finely grate the zest, avoiding the white pith, and set aside.

+ Remove the syrup from the heat, carefully add the vodka and stir in the lemon zest.

+ Pour into the sterilised bottle or jar and leave to infuse for at least 1 day, but up to 3 months. The flavour will develop further the longer you leave it.

+ Once ready, strain the liquid through a fine sieve to remove the zest. Serve freezer cold.

Starters, snacks + soups

'Believe deep down in your heart that you are destined to do great things.'
Joe Paterno

My first experience of soup was the rich, red tomato variety, poured straight from a can, but as I learned more about food, I began to see that there was so much more to soup than that. My idea of a soup is something jam-packed full of taste and texture, with layers and layers of flavour, which can be achieved in a reasonable time span for maximum impact. I love to make large batches of soup and pour some into a flask for part of my laptop lunch. Of course, other light bites such as Aussie Sweetcorn Breakfast Fritters (page 45) are a must when a small meal is desired or as a precursor to a larger one. I wasn't sure where on earth to put my Pizza Expressed Three Ways (page 41), and so placed it in this chapter for a pleasing light bite.

Time from start to finish:
20 minutes (+ ideally 6 hours in the fridge)
Serves: 4
Equipment: Medium frying pan, food processor, 4 x 175ml ramekins

Oil

25g butter

2 shallots

3 garlic cloves

500g chestnut mushrooms

4 tbsp port (optional)

2 sprigs of fresh tarragon

100g cooked chestnuts (available vac packed or tinned from the supermarket)

300g cream cheese

Salt and freshly ground black pepper

Your favourite bread, crackers or breadsticks, to serve

Vegetarian mushroom & port 'faux gras' with tarragon & chestnuts

Great for presents, these will keep in the fridge for up to 4 days. I have been known to give these little bad boys away as part of a hamper at Christmas and they are good to have on hand, year round, as a really tasty snack.

+ Put a drizzle of oil and the butter in a medium frying pan over a low heat.

+ Peel and finely chop the shallots and garlic and add to the pan. Cook for 3 minutes, stirring now and again, until soft and slightly golden.

+ Finely slice the mushrooms. Add them to the pan along with the port, if using, and season with salt and pepper. Turn up the heat to medium and cook for 8 minutes, or until the mushrooms have softened and all their liquid has evaporated.

+ Meanwhile, pick the leaves from one sprig of tarragon, divide the other sprig into four smaller pieces and then roughly chop the chestnuts.

+ Tip the cooked mushroom mixture into a food processor with the chestnuts, individual leaves of tarragon and the cream cheese. Blitz for a few minutes until really smooth, scraping down the sides of the bowl once or twice. Have a taste of it and adjust the seasoning if necessary.

+ Divide between the ramekins, smooth their tops and place a tarragon sprig on top of each to decorate. Arrange them on a small tray or plate, cover with cling film and refrigerate for at least 6 hours or overnight. You can also serve these straight away, but their texture will be much softer and flavour not so intense. Serve with your favourite bread, crackers or breadsticks.

Time from start to finish:
40 minutes (for all three pizza toppings)
or
Dough: 15 minutes prep
Toppings: 5 minutes per pizza
Time baking in the oven:
8–10 minutes
Makes: 3 thin 14 x 40cm pizza bases
Equipment: Large bowl, freestanding electric mixer fitted with the dough hook (optional), rolling pin, 3 baking sheets, clean tea towel (or cling film), scissors, blender, peeler

Pizza dough

300g strong bread flour, plus a little extra for dusting

1 x 7g sachet of fast-action dried yeast

1½ tsp salt

3 tbsp extra virgin olive oil, plus extra for oiling

175ml warm tap water (not too hot)

Pizza expressed three ways

You can either make the dough from scratch for this pizza, which takes no time at all, or for an even speedier method, buy soft tortillas and use those as a base for the pizza instead of making your own.

+ Preheat the oven to 240°C, (fan 220°C), 475°F, Gas Mark 9.

+ Put the flour, yeast and salt into a large bowl and stir to combine. Make a well in the centre and add the oil and the water. Then mix it all together with a wooden spoon to form a soft, slightly sticky ball.

+ At this stage I like to get my hands into the bowl and squidge everything together. Then throw a little flour on the work surface and knead the dough for 8 minutes by hand (or 4 minutes in a freestanding electric mixer fitted with a dough hook).

+ Divide the dough into three equal(ish) pieces and then use a rolling pin to roll each one out into roughly a 14 x 40cm rectangle. It will be really nice and thin. Put each rectangle on an oiled baking sheet and cover with a clean tea towel or some oiled cling film so they do not dry out while you prepare the toppings. There are three delicious toppings on the next page – each recipe provides enough to top one pizza base. You can make one pizza using the topping you like or make three to try each of them!

>

Harissa, chilli & sausage pizza with fennel seed & rocket

2 spring onions
1 red chilli (optional)
2 fat sausages
2 tbsp harissa paste (found in most supermarkets)
2 tsp fennel seed
A handful of wild rocket
Drizzle of extra virgin olive oil
Salt and freshly ground black pepper

Goat's cheese & sweet pepper pizza with chorizo

50ml passata
50g mild or hot Peppadew peppers (jars are available from most supermarkets, near the capers and vinegars!)
3 sprigs of fresh thyme
1 garlic clove
75g goat's cheese
10 chorizo slices
Small handful of fresh basil leaves
Drizzle of extra virgin olive oil
Salt and freshly ground black pepper

Feta, hummus & courgette pizza with balsamic drizzle & mint

100g hummus
100g feta cheese
½ small courgette
6 cherry tomatoes
Drizzle of balsamic glaze (found in the supermarket)
Extra virgin olive oil
Small handful of fresh mint leaves
Salt and freshly ground black pepper

Harissa, chilli & sausage pizza with fennel seed & rocket

+ Trim and finely slice the spring onions (both the green and the white bits), then halve, deseed and finely slice the red chilli, if using, and set aside.

+ Snip the skin off the sausages and then peel it off or squeeze the sausage meat out. Break the sausage meat into small pieces.

+ Spread the harissa paste all over the pizza base. I like to leave a 1cm border, for aesthetic purposes only! Scatter over the onions, chilli, sausage meat and fennel seed and season with a little salt and pepper.

Goat's cheese & sweet pepper pizza with chorizo

+ Put the passata and Peppadew peppers in a blender. Run your fingers down the length of the thyme sprigs to release their leaves, peel the garlic and add both to the blender. Blitz until smooth and then spread over the pizza base, leaving a 1cm border.

+ Break the goat's cheese into small pieces and scatter over the pizza base along with the chorizo slices. Season with a little salt and pepper.

Feta, hummus & courgette pizza with balsamic drizzle & mint

+ Spread the hummus over the base of the pizza and crumble the feta on top. Use a vegetable peeler to slice the courgette into long, thin strips. Keep going until all is used up and arrange these also. Halve the tomatoes, scatter them over and season with salt and pepper.

+ When you have topped the pizzas, bake each one in the oven for 8–10 minutes or until crispy and the sausage on the harissa, chilli & sausage pizza is cooked. Once cooked, scatter the rocket over. Scatter the basil leaves over the cooked goat's cheese pizza and drizzle with a little oil. Drizzle the balsamic glaze over the feta pizza with a good drizzle of olive oil, then scatter over the mint leaves. Serve the pizzas immediately.

Time from start to finish:
20 minutes
Serves: 2
Equipment: Colander, blender
or food processor, medium pan,
large frying pan, medium bowl
or jug

Chilli jam

375g jar of mild or hot Peppadew
peppers
125g cherry tomatoes
½ bag of fresh basil
6 tbsp caster sugar

Fritters

Sunflower oil
50g self-raising flour
50ml whole milk
1 egg
425g tin of sweetcorn
50g half- or full-fat crème fraiche,
to serve

Avocado & rocket salad

1 ripe avocado
½ bag of rocket
Drizzle of extra virgin olive oil
Drizzle of balsamic vinegar
Salt and freshly ground black pepper

Aussie sweetcorn breakfast fritters with avocado & rocket salad & sweet chilli jam

Peppadew peppers, which are used in this dish, are generally found in a jar near the capers in the supermarket. However, if you can't find them, just use 100g of cherry tomatoes in their place (in addition to the cherry tomatoes already in the recipe), along with a bit of Tabasco.

+ First, prepare the chilli jam. Drain the Peppadew peppers well and put them in a blender or food processor with the cherry tomatoes. Rip the leaves from the basil stalks, add them too and blitz until smooth. Then tip into a medium pan over a medium heat. Add the caster sugar and bring to the boil.

+ Meanwhile, start on the fritters. Put a big drizzle of oil into a large frying pan over a medium to high heat. Put the flour, milk and egg in a medium bowl or jug with a big pinch of salt and some pepper. Beat the mixture hard with a wooden spoon to get rid of any lumps. Drain the sweetcorn well, stir into the batter and set aside for a moment.

+ Once the chilli jam is boiling, turn down the heat and leave it to simmer away for 8 minutes, stirring it from time to time so that it does not catch on the bottom.

+ Once the oil in the frying pan is nice and hot, put four dollops of the fritter mix into the pan. Each one should be about 10cm in diameter and this uses all of the mixture up. Cook for about 3 minutes.

+ Meanwhile, cut the avocado in half and remove the stone. The easiest way to get the stone out is to put the blade of a sharp knife into the stone as if you were going to cut it in half. Then twist the knife a bit and the stone should just pop out. Peel off the skin and slice the flesh into long, thin strips. Arrange to one side of two serving plates and set aside for a moment.

>

Simple salmon ceviche with tortilla chips

(continued)

+ Put the tortillas in the oven for 5 minutes. I have a habit of not remembering they are in, though, and so I really have to keep an eye on them!

+ When the tortillas are crisp and golden, remove from the oven and leave to cool for a minute before piling into a serving bowl. Or, if using shop-bought tortilla chips, simply empty them into the serving bowl.

+ When the ceviche is just turning a bit white at the edges, it is ready, so remove it from the fridge. Rip up the mint leaves, scatter them over and serve with the tortilla chips.

Time from start to finish:
20 minutes
Serves: 4
Equipment: Large bowl, zester,
large frying pan, 2 baking trays

225g self-raising flour

3 tbsp soft light brown sugar

1 tsp baking powder

1 tsp ground cinnamon

2 tsp ground ginger

Pinch of salt

½ lemon

½ vanilla pod (or a couple of drops of
vanilla extract) (optional)

300ml semi-skimmed milk

1 medium egg

Sunflower oil

12 slices of Parma ham (or bacon)

To serve

100ml maple syrup

100g sour cream or half- or full-fat
crème fraîche

Gingerbread pancakes with Parma ham & maple syrup

Major brownie points are awarded to anyone who goes the extra mile on Sunday and rustles up this breakfast dish. If you prefer to have the pancakes plain, then just omit the cinnamon, ground ginger, lemon zest, vanilla and sugar; this plain mix can also be used for your Yorkshire puddings.

+ Preheat the oven to 110°C, (fan 90°C), 225°F, Gas Mark ½. This is to keep the pancakes warm, as they are cooked in batches.

+ Put the flour, sugar, baking powder, cinnamon, ginger and salt into a large bowl, give them a quick mix and make a well in the centre. Finely grate the lemon zest in. Split the vanilla pod open, scrape the seeds out and add them too (or vanilla extract, if using). Then gradually pour the milk in bit by bit, stirring all the time to give a smooth mixture. Beat the egg in well and set aside.

+ Put a drizzle of oil into a large frying pan on a medium heat and cook the Parma ham (or bacon) for 2–3 minutes on each side until nice and crisp. Then remove with tongs and drain on kitchen paper. Tip onto a baking tray and keep warm in the oven until ready to serve.

+ Leave the pan on the heat, but reduce it to low and add a little bit more oil if need be. Then spoon in four dollops of the pancake mix (to spread to about 10cm wide). Leave to cook for 1–2 minutes until golden, then flip them over and cook for another 1–2 minutes. Slide them onto a baking tray and put in the oven to keep warm. Then repeat with the remaining mix to give 12 in total.

+ Once you have made all of the pancakes, divide them between four plates. I like to pile the Parma ham high on them, drizzle with the maple syrup and serve with a dollop of sour cream or crème fraîche.

Time from start to finish:
25 minutes
Serves: 2
Equipment: Large roasting tin,
medium pan

500g baby or new potatoes

Olive oil

400g tin of chopped tomatoes

4 tbsp balsamic vinegar

1–2 tsp smoked paprika

1–2 tsp caster sugar

150ml aïoli (shop-bought, or if
you fancy making your own,
see page 163)

150g chorizo ring

A small handful of fresh flat leaf
parsley

Salt and freshly ground black pepper

Roasted new patatas & chorizo bravas with aïoli

I went to a restaurant with my dad where we feasted on spicy patatas bravas, jamón ibérico that melted on the tongue like a fine butter and garlic prawns served simply with lime and fresh herbs. My dad (the Spanish teacher) was talking to the waiter who thought his Spanish was so good he was actually from Spain. Well, I just sat there beaming with pride. This is a recipe to remind me of that fantastic Friday lunch. There are many ways to make patatas bravas, and chorizo is not usually thrown in, but being a chorizo addict, totally entranced by its robust flavours, I just had to add some.

+ Preheat the oven to 220°C, (fan 200°C), 425°F, Gas Mark 7.

+ Put the potatoes into a large roasting tin. If using new potatoes (not 'baby'), halve or quarter them first. Season with salt and pepper and drizzle with a good amount of oil. Roast in the hot oven for 20 minutes.

+ Pour the tomatoes into a medium pan over a medium heat. Add the vinegar, paprika and sugar to taste, a drizzle of oil, and salt and pepper. Bring to a simmer then bubble away for 15 minutes, stirring occasionally.

+ Meanwhile, make your aïoli and set aside or skip to the next step if using shop-bought.

+ Peel and chop the chorizo into chunky pieces and set aside.

+ Give the sauce a stir and check on the potatoes, tossing them about a bit. Add the chorizo to the sauce for the last 5 minutes of cooking time.

+ The potatoes are cooked when crisp and golden outside and tender inside when pierced with a knife. Remove them from the oven and tip onto a serving platter for sharing. Take the now-reduced tomato sauce off the heat and add some salt and pepper if need be. Then pour it over the potatoes and top with the aïoli and tear over the parsley leaves. Sometimes in Spain this is served with cocktail sticks. Wonderful!

Time from start to finish:
35 minutes
Serves: 4
Equipment: Large pan, small
frying pan, stick or standard
blender, scissors

50g butter

2 large leeks

2 large floury potatoes

100ml white wine

1 litre good-quality chicken stock (fresh is best to use here)

75g oak-smoked bacon lardons or cubed pancetta

A little double cream (optional)

Small handful of fresh chives

Salt and freshly ground black pepper

Potato & leek vichyssoise with crispy bacon & chives

It has been said that this soup comes from Vichy in France, but rumour has it that the chef who created it had some Vichy roots and the link is no more than that. It is supposed to be served cold, but personally I am not one for cold potato soup. So I turned up the heat and added one of my favourite ingredients, bacon, which has been crisped up to within a very inch of its life, adding some welcome crunch and saltiness, along with a drizzle of cream and a few snips of chives.

+ Put a large pan on a low heat with the butter. While it is heating up, trim the leeks, remove any tough outer leaves, split them in half lengthways and wash really well before finely slicing. Add to the pan and cook gently for about 10 minutes until really soft, stirring from time to time.

+ Meanwhile, peel and chop the potatoes into bite-sized chunks. Add to the leeks (once they are cooked) along with the wine. Allow the wine to bubble down for 2–3 minutes before adding the stock and some salt and pepper. Then turn up the heat and bring to the boil. Let the soup bubble away for 10–15 minutes until the potato is nice and tender.

+ While the soup is cooking, place a small frying pan on a high heat. Once hot, add the bacon (or pancetta) lardons and fry for 3–4 minutes, stirring from time to time, until crisp and golden. Spoon onto kitchen paper to drain, and set aside.

+ Using a stick blender, carefully blitz the now-cooked soup until really smooth. A jug blender does the trick also; just be careful to blend in a couple of batches.

+ Taste the soup, adding more salt and pepper if you think it needs it (but allowing for the saltiness of the bacon) and then ladle into four serving bowls. Swirl a little cream on top of each, if using, snip the chives over and finally scatter with the cooked lardons to serve.

Time from start to finish:
20 minutes
Serves: 4
Equipment: **Large pan or wok**

Vegetable oil

1 lemongrass stalk

2 garlic cloves

5cm piece of fresh ginger

Large handful of fresh coriander

3 kaffir lime leaves (fresh, frozen or dried)

2 x 400ml tins of coconut milk

300ml good-quality chicken stock (fresh is best to use here)

1 red chilli

3 skinless, boneless chicken breasts

1 bunch of spring onions

2 limes

2–3 tbsp fish sauce

1–2 tsp caster sugar

Salt and freshly ground black pepper

Thai chicken soup with coconut milk & ginger

A smoother-than-velvet Thai-style soup with an orchestra of flavours going on inside. If you can get your hands on fresh kaffir lime leaves that would be great; the dried ones can be found in the herbs and spices section in the supermarket, or use frozen.

+ Heat a drizzle of oil in a large pan or wok on a medium heat.

+ Trim the lemongrass stalk and discard any tough outer leaves before finely chopping the white bit (discard the green bit as it can be quite bitter). Peel and finely chop the garlic and then peel the ginger and cut it into thin slivers. Chop the stalks off the coriander (in one go) and then finely slice them (keeping the coriander leaves aside for later).

+ Carefully toss them all in the hot oil with the kaffir lime leaves and stir-fry for a couple of minutes, being careful that nothing catches and burns.

+ Next add the coconut milk and stock and leave to come to the boil.

+ Meanwhile, halve the chilli lengthways and then finely slice it, leaving the seeds in if you like it quite fiery. Chop the chicken into bite-sized pieces and add both ingredients to the now-boiled soup. Reduce the heat a little and leave it to bubble away for about 8 minutes until the chicken is cooked.

+ Finely slice the spring onions (both the green and the white bits), juice the limes and roughly chop half of the reserved coriander leaves. Add these once the chicken is cooked and then leave to simmer for a final minute. Finally, add enough fish sauce and sugar to taste and season with salt and pepper if necessary.

+ Ladle into four serving bowls, scatter the remaining coriander leaves over and serve.

Time from start to finish:
15 minutes
Serves: 2
Equipment: Medium pan with lid

Hot-and-sour king prawn soup

A light, lucid soup with fragrant Asian flavours and succulent blushing prawns. Definitely one for a packed lunch.

500ml good-quality fish or chicken stock (fresh is best to use here)

1–2 red chillies (depending on how hot you like them)

1 lemongrass stalk

Small handful of fresh coriander

2 kaffir lime leaves (fresh, frozen or dried)

3 tbsp fish sauce

12 sustainably caught raw king prawns, shell off

2 limes

1–2 tsp caster sugar

+ Pour the stock into a medium pan on a high heat and cover with the lid (so it heats up more quickly).

+ Meanwhile, slice, deseed and finely chop the chillies, finely slice the lemongrass (the white bit only) and coriander stalks (reserving the leaves).

+ Once the stock has come to the boil, add them to the pan along with the kaffir lime leaves and fish sauce and cover again with the lid. Turn the heat down a little and leave to simmer for 4–5 minutes.

+ Add the prawns and continue to simmer for another minute or so until the prawns turn pink.

+ Then finish with the coriander leaves, juice of the limes and sugar to taste.

+ Ladle into two serving bowls and serve.

Time from start to finish:
15 minutes
Chilling time: 30 minutes in the
freezer (or 1 hour in the fridge)
Serves: 4–6
Equipment: Blender or food
processor, large jug, baking tray

Gazpacho

1kg ripe vine-ripened tomatoes

2 red peppers

1 garlic clove

½ bag of fresh basil

6 tbsp extra virgin olive oil

4 tsp sherry vinegar

A few shakes of Tabasco sauce

Pinch of sugar

5cm piece of cucumber

Handful of ice cubes

Croutons

1 ciabatta roll (about 90g)

Extra virgin olive oil

Salt and freshly ground black pepper

Red pepper, tomato & basil gazpacho with salt & pepper croutons

Every summer I book myself and the family on Britain's favourite orange airline and head south to Spain. Circling high above Barcelona's La Rambla, which leads down to the sparkling sapphire blue surf, I know that very soon I will be among the bustling throng of beautiful bronzed bodies, sipping on a bubbling cava, dipping hunks of just-cooked bread in hot sizzling oil full of garlicky prawns and diving my spoon into a perfect bowl of that intensely flavoured, cooling Spanish soup.

+ Preheat the oven to 200°C, (fan 180°C), 400°F, Gas Mark 6.

+ Roughly chop the tomatoes, halve and deseed the peppers, snapping them into a few pieces, and peel the garlic. Pick the leaves from the basil stalks, reserve a small handful for garnish and put the rest in a blender or food processor with the tomatoes, peppers and garlic. Then add the oil, sherry vinegar, Tabasco, sugar and some salt and pepper and blitz until as smooth as possible.

+ Taste, adding a little more Tabasco or seasoning if you think it needs it. Pour into a large jug, cover with cling film and put in the freezer for 30 minutes (or the fridge for 1 hour) to cool right down.

+ Cut the ciabatta up into bite-sized cubes, scatter them on a baking tray, drizzle with oil and season with salt and pepper. Bake in the oven for about 6 minutes.

+ Meanwhile, cut the cucumber into little cubes and set these aside.

+ Remove the croutons from the oven once they are crisp and golden and set aside until ready to serve.

+ When ready to serve, divide the soup between the serving bowls. Sprinkle the cucumber over, pop a few ice cubes in each one, scatter the croutons and reserved basil on top and drizzle with a little oil.

Starters, snacks + soups

Time from start to finish:
30 minutes
Serves: 6
Equipment: Large pan with lid, 2
small bowls, baking tray, blender

Soup

Vegetable oil

1 large leek

1 large potato

900ml good-quality chicken stock
(fresh is best to use here)

1 whole head of broccoli

150g strong blue cheese, such as
Stilton or Roquefort

Accompaniments

3 garlic cloves

Small handful of fresh chives

50g softened butter

1 French baguette

6 tbsp mascarpone

Salt and freshly ground black pepper

Broccoli & blue cheese soup with chive mascarpone & warm garlic bread

Roquefort is the cheese to go for if you like this super strong, or you can keep it British with some good old Stilton. Either way, I really like the combination of a blue cheese with some broccoli – definitely one of my top 10 favourite flavour combos. A lovely filling winter soup.

+ Put a drizzle of oil into a large pan over a medium heat and while this heats up, top and tail the leek, discarding most of the dark green bit. Then slit it lengthways, discard the hard outer leaves and wash under the cold tap. Finely slice and add to the pan, then give them a stir and leave to cook for about 10 minutes.

+ Meanwhile, prepare the garlic butter. Peel and finely chop the garlic and finely chop the chives. Put all of the garlic and half of the chives into a small bowl with the softened butter and some salt and pepper. Mix and set aside.

+ Returning to the soup, peel and chop the potato into 1cm cubes and add to the softened leeks, along with the chicken stock. Turn up the heat and put the lid on to help bring it up to the boil quickly.

+ Once this is boiling remove the lid, reduce the heat a little and leave to simmer away for 10 minutes or so.

+ Preheat the oven to 180°C, (fan 160°C), 350°F, Gas Mark 4 for the garlic bread.

+ Roughly chop the broccoli (including the stalk) and add to the soup for the last 5 minutes or so.

+ Now, divide the baguette into three even-sized pieces and split each one in half as if you were making a sandwich. Pop the bread, cut side up, on

>

Broccoli & blue cheese soup with chive mascarpone & warm garlic bread

(continued)

a baking tray and put in the oven for 5 minutes. (I have to really keep an eye on it as I sometimes don't remember that it is in there!)

+ Meanwhile, put the remaining chives in a small bowl with the mascarpone. Season with salt and pepper and stir together once (otherwise it might go grainy), then set aside.

+ Remove the toasted bread from the oven, slather the cut sides with the garlic butter and return it to the oven for a further 4–5 minutes.

+ Once the soup is ready, check the potatoes and broccoli are cooked through and remove from the heat. Carefully blend the soup until smooth. Crumble in the blue cheese, give the soup another quick blitz and then season to taste.

+ Divide the soup between six serving bowls. Add a dollop of the chive mascarpone to each. Remove the garlic bread from the oven and serve a piece with each one.

Time from start to finish:
40 minutes
Serves: 4
Equipment: Large pan with
lid, food processor fitted with
the slicing blade attachment
(optional), baking sheet, grater

Vegetable oil

Knob of butter

4 big onions

1 bay leaf

2 garlic cloves

Small handful of fresh sage leaves

1 tbsp plain flour

1 litre good-quality beef stock

Small handful of fresh flat leaf parsley

Croutons

1 demi-baguette

75g Gruyère cheese (or Parmesan
works well too)

Big pinch of English mustard powder

Salt and freshly ground black pepper

French onion & sage soup with big fat Gruyère & mustard croutons

I really do love a good bowl of French onion soup. Of course the best soups are made with the very best stock: a rich, thick beef stock that has been cooked for hours, so deep in flavour I could do a little dance. This is best made with a fresh stock from the butcher, but a supermarket one (not from concentrate) will do just fine too. I sometimes stick the cooked soup in a flask to have when I am on the go. A lovely luscious lunchtime treat.

+ Place a large pan on a medium heat with a drizzle of oil and the butter. Peel and very finely slice the onions. This is a bit of a task, but using a food processor fitted with the slicing blade attachment should make things a bit easier.

+ Add the onions to the pan with the bay leaf, pop the lid on and leave to cook for about 25 minutes until soft. Give them a good stir every now and then so they don't burn. If they look like they are catching at any time, just add a little more oil.

+ Meanwhile, peel and finely chop the garlic, then finely chop the sage leaves and set both aside.

+ Preheat the oven to 150°C, (fan 130°C), 300°F, Gas Mark 2. Trim the baguette ends, cut it into eight thick slices (about 2.5cm thick) and lay them out on a baking sheet.

+ Next, roughly grate the Gruyère cheese (or Parmesan), sprinkle the mustard powder over, if using, and toss it all about to mix together. Then spread it evenly over the tops of the bread slices.

+ Check on the onions, giving them a good stir every now and then.

>

French onion & sage soup with big fat Gruyère & mustard croutons

(continued)

+ Once the onions are a few minutes off being ready, place the croutons into the oven to bake for about 4–5 minutes. You could also grill them for about 5 minutes if you prefer.

+ Once the onions are lovely and soft, add the garlic, sage and flour, giving them a good stir in. Pour in the beef stock, put the lid back on, increase the heat and bring the soup up to the boil. Then leave it to bubble away for 2–3 minutes before removing it from the heat. Season to taste with salt and pepper.

+ Remove the crisp, melted-cheese-topped croutons from the oven. Pick and roughly chop the parsley leaves.

+ Divide the soup between four wide serving bowls and serve with the croutons either sitting right on top of the soup or to the side of the bowl. Scatter the parsley over and serve.

Salads

'I am easily satisfied with the very best.'
Winston Churchill

I remember when a salad used to be a not-so-pretty-looking piece of iceberg lettuce, a few slivers of cucumber with a plump, round tomato quartered and scattered on top. Oh, how things have moved on! There is an incredible array of salad leaves, veg and even fruit now available since those heady days of big Afros and flared trousers, and in order to counterbalance my penchant for all things sweet, I tend to whip up a fast and fresh salad several times a week.

Time from start to finish:
20 minutes
Serves: 4
Equipment: Large serving platter

2 x 250g packs of ready-prepared mango cubes (or 2 large ripe mangoes)

200g feta cheese

4 radishes

1 ripe avocado

Small handful of fresh basil

1 bag of pea shoots (or wild rocket)

A drizzle of a really good extra virgin olive oil

1 lime

Salt and freshly ground black pepper

Mango, feta & avocado salad with fresh lime juice

Mangoes are not the cheapest things to buy, and nor is their comrade the avocado pear. But once in a while, a tasty tropical treat for me is a necessity. In one of the many places that I love, Sri Lanka, the avocados grow in abundance. Early in the morning, I would wake up, grab my friend and stand ready under the avo tree. After a gentle shake, dozens of these emerald green fruits would come tumbling to the ground. Sitting in my kitchen back in London with the holiday blues, I devised this recipe as a way of transporting me back to the exotic, calming world that is Sri Lanka's southern coast. I found the pea shoots in the supermarket near me – they are little baby leaves, very cute and tasty. If you can't find them, wild rocket is fine to use instead.

+ Tip the mango onto a large serving platter. (I do love some prepared mango, at times!) Or if using whole mangoes, slice the two cheeks off either side of the stone. Cut them in half and then run the knife through the flesh close to the skin to peel it, as you would with a melon. Dice the flesh into bite-sized pieces and scatter onto the big serving platter. I like to go back and slice off the remaining skinny bits of mango and do the same thing with them so as not to waste any.

+ Crumble the feta cheese over. Top and tail the radishes and then slice them as fine as you can get them before scattering them over also.

+ Cut the avocado in half and discard the stone. I put the blade of a knife into it and then give it a twist – the stone usually comes out beautifully. Then carefully peel away the skin and slice or dice up the avocado and add to the salad.

+ Tear the basil leaves from the stalks and scatter the leaves over with the pea shoots (or rocket). Season with salt and pepper, drizzle with oil and finish by squeezing the lime juice over.

Time from start to finish:
20 minutes
Serves: 2
Equipment: Small frying pan,
small bowl, small plate

50g walnut pieces

150g seedless red grapes

2 celery sticks

2 Granny Smith apples

Small handful of fresh flat leaf parsley
or dill

50g dried cranberries (or raisins)

Dressing

100g Greek yogurt (full fat, low fat or
no fat)

1–2 tsp honey

1 tsp Dijon mustard

Salt and freshly ground black pepper

Wild Waldorf salad with toasted walnuts & Granny Smiths

I am not sure why I named this salad 'wild'; it must have been my frame of mind at the time or perhaps I was just in search of a suitable alliteration! I always double up this recipe so I can have it throughout the week as a packed lunch, or it's delicious served with some pan-fried chicken. I usually take a skinless, boneless chicken breast, bash it until it's about 5mm thick, squish it in some thyme, salt and pepper and then fry until cooked. I leave the chicken to cool, then pop it on top of my wild Waldorf salad in my plastic lunch box.

+ Put a small frying pan on a low to medium heat, with no oil, for the walnuts. While waiting for that to heat up, get on with the dressing.

+ Spoon the Greek yogurt into a small bowl and add the honey (to taste) and Dijon mustard. Mix them together well, season to taste with salt and pepper and set aside.

+ Tip the walnuts into the now-hot pan and leave to toast for 2–3 minutes, tossing them about occasionally so they don't burn.

+ Meanwhile, wash and halve the grapes, finely slice the celery and throw them into a medium salad-serving bowl.

+ Remove the walnuts from the heat, tipping them onto a small plate to stop them from toasting further, and leave them to cool down for a bit.

+ Quarter the apples, remove their cores, chop them into bite-sized chunks and add them to the serving bowl. Then pick and roughly chop the parsley or dill leaves and throw them in along with the cranberries (or raisins). Then add the walnuts, crumbling any that are large.

+ Tip the dressing into the salad, stir everything together, season to taste, adding a little more honey, herbs or salt and pepper if you think it needs it, and serve.

Time from start to finish:
20 minutes
Serves: 4–6
Equipment: Kettle, mug or small
bowl, zester, colander, medium
pan, peeler

400g tin of cannellini beans

250g bunch of asparagus

3 courgettes

1 perfectly ripe avocado

Olive oil

1 bag of wild rocket

Small handful of fresh mint

Small handful of fresh basil

Handful of toasted pine nuts (about
25g) (they come ready-toasted from
the supermarket)

25g Parmesan cheese

Dressing

1 small red chilli or a pinch of dried
chilli flakes (optional)

1 lemon

4 tbsp extra virgin olive oil

Couple of squidges of honey

Salt and freshly ground black pepper

Courgette 'pappardelle' with asparagus, avocado salad & rocket

A lovely, light laptop lunch which will become the envy
of your colleagues, or a simple inviting supper dish.

+ Put the kettle on to boil.

+ Meanwhile, make the dressing. Deseed and finely chop the chilli (if using)
and add to a mug or small bowl, or simply add the dried chilli flakes.
Finely grate the lemon zest in and squeeze in the juice. Add the oil and
honey and season with salt and pepper. Whisk together with a fork.
Next, drain and rinse the cannellini beans, toss them through the dressing
and set aside.

+ Pour the now-boiled water and a big pinch of salt into a medium pan
and put on a high heat to bring the water back up to the boil. Trim the
ends off the asparagus where they look dried out and add to the water to
cook for 4 minutes.

+ Using a peeler, take a strip off the length of a courgette to look like
'pappardelle'. Keep going in the same place until you have peeled away
half of the courgette, then flip it over and do the same with the other side.
You now don't need the bit that is left when you've peeled away all you
can, but you could save it for use in a soup or stir-fry. Repeat with the
remaining courgettes.

+ Once the asparagus is just tender, remove it from the water with a slotted
spoon and rinse under cold running water for a minute or so until cool.
Then set aside. Now add the courgette 'pappardelle' to the boiling water
and cook for about 3 minutes.

+ Meanwhile, quarter, de-stone and peel the avocado. Cut it lengthways
into 1cm-thick slices, drizzle with oil (so they don't go brown) and
set aside.

+ Once the courgettes are just tender, drain them in the colander and rinse
under cold running water until cool. Drain well and toss a drizzle of oil
through to stop them from sticking together.

>

Courgette 'pappardelle' with asparagus, avocado salad & rocket

(continued)

+ Now to assemble. Tip the rocket onto a large serving platter. Scatter the courgette and asparagus over. Rip the leaves from the mint and basil stalks and sprinkle them over with the pine nuts. Give everything a little toss about with your hands and then arrange the avocado on top. Spoon the cannellini beans and dressing over and then shave the Parmesan on top using the peeler and serve.

Time from start to finish:
20 minutes
Serves: 4
Equipment: Large frying pan,
small bowl, colander, large bowl,
large plate, pestle and mortar
(or mug and rolling pin)

Vegetable oil

4 rump or sirloin steaks, about 2cm
thick (about 600g in total)

1 head of romaine lettuce

Large handful of fresh coriander

Large handful of fresh mint

Small handful of fresh basil

50g salted, roasted peanuts (not dry
roasted)

Dressing

1 hot red chilli

2cm piece of fresh ginger

1 garlic clove

2 large or 3 small limes

2 tbsp vegetable oil

1 tbsp fish sauce

Large squidge of honey

Salt and freshly ground black pepper

Thai beef salad with roasted peanuts & chilli dressing

A super-easy, super-simple and, dare I say it, pretty healthy salad. Great for those last days of summer or for a light autumnal meal. I like to use rump steak, but sirloin or even fillet, if you are going for it, will do.

+ Put a large frying pan on a high heat with a drizzle of oil. Season the steaks well with a good amount of salt and pepper. This will give the steaks a tasty crust once cooked. Add them to the hot oil and leave to cook, untouched, for 3–4 minutes, depending on how well you like them done.

+ Meanwhile, get on with the dressing. Halve and deseed the chilli, peel the ginger and garlic and then finely chop everything. Place in a small bowl and squeeze the lime juice over. Add the oil, fish sauce and honey, beat together with a fork, season with salt and pepper to taste and then leave to infuse.

+ Once the steaks have cooked for 3–4 minutes, flip them over and cook for another 3–4 minutes while you prepare the salad.

+ Trim the end off the romaine lettuce, separate the leaves and discard the very centre. Tip into a colander, rinse well and then gently pat dry with kitchen paper. Stack the leaves together and then cut into about 1cm thick slices and place in a large bowl.

+ Bunch the coriander, mint and basil together, rip off the leafy tops and add to the bowl also. (I keep stalks for stocks and soups. They freeze really well and can be used straight from frozen.)

+ Remove the now-cooked steaks from the pan and leave to rest on a large plate, loosely covered with tin foil, for about 5 minutes.

+ Meanwhile, roughly grind the peanuts with a pestle and mortar and set aside. Alternatively, just put them in a mug and use the end of a rolling pin instead.

>

Thai beef salad
with roasted peanuts
& chilli dressing

(continued)

+ Pour half of the dressing onto the salad leaves and toss together well. Then divide them between four serving plates. Take half of the nuts and sprinkle them over the salad.

+ Remove the fat from the steaks and then slice the meat into slices about 1cm thick. Arrange them on top of the salad, sprinkle with the remaining nuts, drizzle with the rest of the dressing and then serve.

Time from start to finish:
15 minutes
Serves: 4
Equipment: Small pan, baking
sheet, mini blender, grater,
colander, really large bowl,
small frying pan

4 medium eggs

¼ French baguette

Extra virgin olive oil

1 garlic clove

20g Parmesan cheese

8 tbsp mayonnaise

3 anchovies (the sort that come in tins
or jars)

½ lime

2 x 340g romaine lettuce heads

225g sustainably caught raw peeled
prawns

2 tbsp pomegranate seeds (optional,
you can find them pre-prepared at the
supermarket)

Salt and freshly ground black pepper

Prawn Caesar salad with olive oil croutons & pomegranates

A very scrumptious salad. Sometimes I like to put all of the salad (undressed) in a plastic container and take the dressing in a separate small one. A really good alternative to sandwiches in the middle of the day or a lighter bite for dinner.

+ Turn the oven on to 200°C, (fan 180°C), 400°F, Gas Mark 6.

+ Place the eggs in a small pan and cover with water. Put on a high heat and as soon as the water comes to the boil, let it bubble away for 4 minutes for almost hard-boiled eggs.

+ Cut the baguette into approximately 2cm-square croutons, toss them on a baking sheet, drizzle generously with oil and pop them into the oven for about 6 minutes.

+ Meanwhile, peel and roughly chop the garlic and place in a mini blender. Finely grate the Parmesan and add it along with the mayonnaise and anchovies, then squeeze in the lime juice. Whiz until really smooth and creamy, season with salt and pepper to taste and set aside.

+ Toss the croutons about a bit and return for the remaining cooking time (if not already done).

+ As soon as the eggs are ready, drain them in a colander and run cold water over them for a couple of minutes to stop them cooking.

+ Meanwhile, trim the end off the lettuces, wash and pat the leaves dry with kitchen paper or a clean tea towel and then rip up them up into big pieces and put in a really large bowl.

+ Put a drizzle of oil in a small frying pan on a low heat.

+ Peel the now-cold eggs, quarter them and set aside.

+ The croutons should now be crisp and golden, so remove them from the oven and set aside.

>

Prawn Caesar salad with olive oil croutons & pomegranates

(continued)

+ Turn the heat up to high under the frying pan and add the prawns, season well with salt and pepper and cook for 2–3 minutes until they turn pink and are cooked through.

+ Finally, pour the dressing all over the lettuce and toss gently using two large spoons. Divide between the serving plates, then spoon the prawns over, nestle the egg wedges around, scatter the croutons on top with the pomegranate seeds, if using, and serve.

Time from start to finish:
20 minutes
Serves: 4
Equipment: Kettle, mug or small
bowl, medium pan, colander,
small bowl

300g baby or new potatoes

100g bag of salad leaves, like spinach
or lamb's lettuce

1 head of chicory

250g pack of cooked beetroot (comes
in a vac pack from the fruit and veg
section of the supermarket)

50g capers

1 Granny Smith apple

½ lime

300g pack of hot-smoked mackerel
(with or without peppercorns)

50g roasted hazelnuts (available from
supermarkets ready roasted)

Dressing

Small handful of fresh dill

4 tbsp horseradish sauce

2 tbsp half- or full-fat crème fraîche

1 lime

Squeeze of honey (optional)

Salt and freshly ground black pepper

Mackerel salad with horseradish crème fraîche

One of my favourite foods, which I love served whole, is mackerel. Its opalescent skin slashed, the fresh fish lightly grilled and then served with a tart gooseberry sauce; or smoked mackerel in a salad, straight from the packet. A large dollop of horseradish sauce can stand up to this intensely flavoured fish with some tart Granny Smith apples to cut through its inviting fattiness.

+ Put the kettle on to boil.

+ Meanwhile, make the dressing for the salad. Pick and finely chop the dill leaves and add half to a mug or small bowl (reserving the rest for later). Mix in the horseradish sauce, crème fraîche, enough lime juice to taste and honey (if using). Season to taste with salt and pepper and set aside.

+ Wash the potatoes, tip into a medium pan with a little salt and cover with the now-boiled water. Leave to bubble away for about 15 minutes.

+ Tip the salad leaves onto each of four serving plates or one large serving platter. Trim the end off the chicory, separate the leaves and scatter them over, discarding any damaged outer leaves.

+ Drain the beetroot and cut into small wedges. Rinse and drain the capers. Quarter and core the apple and then slice it into matchsticks. Toss it in a small bowl with the lime juice and then scatter it over the leaves with the beetroot and capers.

+ Peel the skin from the back of the mackerel, remove the dark brown meat and then break the flesh into large chunks and arrange on top of the salad.

+ Check the potatoes are now tender, then drain them off well and leave to cool for a moment.

+ Roughly chop the hazelnuts and scatter over the salad. Nestle the potatoes in now also. Drizzle the dressing back and forth over the salad, scatter the remaining dill on top with a twist of black pepper and serve.

Time from start to finish:
20 minutes
Serves: 4
Equipment: Small pan, colander,
mug or small bowl, peeler

4 medium eggs

2 bags of spinach and rocket salad

½ small red onion

½ cucumber

2 handfuls of pitted black olives (about 100g)

400g tin of butter beans

200g sundried (or sun blush) tomatoes

4 hot-smoked trout fillets (or smoked mackerel fillets, steamed salmon fillets or hot-smoked salmon fillets)

25g Parmesan cheese (optional)

A few sprigs of fresh dill

Dressing

4 tbsp extra virgin olive oil

2 tbsp white wine vinegar (balsamic will also work)

A tiny squeeze of honey (optional)

Pinch of English mustard powder

Salt and freshly ground black pepper

Nifty Niçoise salad with hot-smoked trout & sundried tomatoes

The first time I spotted this on the menu, I asked what was the salad 'Nic-o-ez'. After a look of pity, a raised eyebrow and a helping hand with the correct pronunciation, I dived in to my very first salade Niçoise. I have adapted the traditional recipe, adding some abundantly flavoured trout and doing away with the ever-present tattie in favour of some creamy butter beans.

+ Place the eggs in a small pan and cover with water. Put on a high heat and as soon as the water comes to the boil, let it bubble away for 4 minutes for almost hard-boiled eggs.

+ Meanwhile, divide the salad leaves between four serving plates. Peel and finely slice the red onion, slice up the cucumber and scatter these over the salad leaves along with the olives.

+ Drain and rinse the butter beans well, halve the sundried (or sun blush) tomatoes and arrange these on top also.

+ As soon as the eggs have had their cooking time, drain in the colander and run cold water over them for a couple of minutes to stop them cooking further.

+ Meanwhile, make the dressing for the salad. Put the oil, vinegar, honey, if using, mustard powder and some salt and pepper in a mug or small bowl. Mix together with a fork and set aside.

+ Peel and quarter the now-cold eggs and arrange them on the salad. Either lay the smoked fish fillets on whole or break them into pieces over each salad. Drizzle the dressing over, shave the Parmesan on top using a peeler, rip up the dill, scatter over, then serve, looking out for any small bones in the trout.

The Union cobb

Time from start to finish:
15 minutes
Serves: 4
Equipment: Colander

400g tin of kidney beans

200g cherry tomatoes

2 ready cooked chicken breasts

50g pack of precooked crispy bacon

150g blue cheese

1 ripe avocado

Olive oil

1 lime

250g pack of ready-prepared mango cubes

Salt and freshly ground black pepper

For the ease of making this salad, I have used ingredients that are precooked and prepacked. Of course, if you are not a fan of those kinds of supermarket products, then cook the chicken breasts and the bacon yourself. For an impromptu dish that I have found really does impress, then it's ready-to-go products for me, but when time permits, I make everything from scratch. The ingredients below are my favourite for a cobb, but if you fancy something different, just go ahead and throw it in.

+ First, prepare all the ingredients, keeping them separate as you go. Drain and rinse the kidney beans. Halve the tomatoes and cut the chicken breasts into small bite-sized chunks. Use scissors to snip the crispy bacon into small pieces. Crumble the blue cheese. Halve the avocado, remove the stone, peel off the skin and dice it into cubes, then drizzle them with a little bit of oil or squeeze some lime juice over so they do not go brown and now we are ready to go.

+ Arrange the ingredients (including the already prepared mango) in whichever way tickles your fancy. I like to create a British flag (very patriotic!), but you could arrange them in stripes or rings or layered up in a jar, for example. Even putting everything in a bowl and tossing it all together works too. Then squeeze over more lime juice, drizzle with oil, season with salt and pepper and serve.

Chicken + duck mains

'Laughter is brightest where food is best.'
Irish proverb

My mealtime fallback seems to be chicken. A dash to
the local supermarket to grab some chicken breasts or
thighs off the shelves, then a quick rush home to whip
something up. I used to just prepare the same repertoire
of meals, the same old failsafes that I always make
without thinking. Those dishes and family favourites
are great and serve an important purpose, but I really
wanted to try and add to that repertoire to give people
even more variety for their daily meals. The good thing
with poultry is that it can take lots of flavour, so when I
am testing with it, I can have lots of fun, adding a touch
of spice here or a bit of tang there, mixing it all up with
layers of flavours.

Whole roast perky peri peri chicken

Prep time (before and after cooking): **30 minutes**
Time roasting in the oven: **1 hour 50 minutes (depending on the size of bird)**
Serves: **4**
Equipment: **Large roasting tin, small bowl, grater, large plate, medium ovenproof dish, mug or small bowl**

2kg whole chicken, preferably free range and/or organic
150ml water, chicken stock or red wine

Peri peri sauce
5 garlic cloves
1–5 red chillies (as hot as you dare!)
2cm piece of fresh ginger
50ml vegetable oil
25ml white or red wine vinegar
3 tbsp soy sauce
1–2 tbsp Tabasco sauce (again, as hot as you dare!)
2 tbsp smoked paprika
3 tsp dried oregano
1 tsp caster sugar (optional)
1 lime

Vegetables
3 red onions
500g baby new potatoes

Salad
1 lime
1 tsp caster sugar (or a squidge of honey)
3 tbsp extra virgin olive oil
1 bag of crispy salad leaves
Salt and freshly ground black pepper

A different way to roast chicken. A 1.5–1.8kg chicken would be about enough to serve four people, but I have given the recipe a bigger bird so that there is some meat left over for sandwiches the next day. If you use a different size to the one here, work out the cooking time based on 20 minutes per 450g, plus 20 minutes. Regardless of what size bird you use, add the onions and potatoes about 45 minutes before the end of the cooking time. To speed up the cooking process, use some good sharp scissors to snip the chicken along the backbone to splay it out and cook flat.

+ Preheat the oven to 200°C, (fan 180°C), 400°F, Gas Mark 6. Sit the chicken in a large roasting tin and season well with salt and pepper and drizzle with oil. Place in the oven and cook for 1 hour, and meanwhile prepare the peri peri sauce.

+ Peel and roughly chop the garlic, halve, deseed and finely chop the chillies and place both in a small bowl. Finely grate in the ginger (unpeeled) and then add the oil, vinegar, soy sauce, Tabasco, smoked paprika, oregano and sugar (if using). Finely grate in the lime zest and then squeeze in the juice and mix altogether.

+ Remove the chicken from the oven after 1 hour and tip three-quarters of the peri peri sauce onto it, spreading it all over with the back of a spoon. Peel and quarter the onions, leaving the roots intact, and toss them in around the chicken along with the potatoes. Season them with salt and pepper and then return to the oven to cook for the final 50 or so minutes. At the end of the cooking time the chicken will most likely look burnt, but worry not, as this is the peri peri style.

>

Whole roast perky peri peri chicken
(continued)

+ To check the chicken is cooked, pierce the thickest part of a thigh with the point of a sharp knife and the juices should run clear. Check the meat has no pinkness remaining either and that it is completely cooked through. Once cooked, carefully lift the chicken from the roasting tin onto a large plate and cover it loosely with tin foil so it can rest and become juicier. Using a slotted spoon, remove the vegetables from the tin also, transferring them to a medium ovenproof dish. Then put them back in the oven (with the oven now turned off) to keep warm.

+ Carefully pour the oil out from the roasting tin, leaving the juices and sticky bits behind. Put it on a medium heat and add the remaining sauce and 150ml of water, stock or red wine. Allow to simmer for a few minutes, scraping up all the sticky bits from the bottom.

+ Meanwhile, prepare the salad. Squeeze the lime juice into a mug or small bowl and add the sugar (or honey), oil and a little salt and pepper. Give it a good whisk up. Tip the salad leaves into a large salad-serving bowl, pour the dressing over and toss the leaves about.

+ Returning to the chicken, pour any juices on the plate into the sauce before carving the meat up. Arrange on serving plates with the roasted onions and potatoes. Serve with the dressed salad and the sauce in a small jug.

Really simple Sri Lankan chicken curry with coconut milk & cashew nut rice

Time from start to finish:
20 minutes
Serves: 4
Equipment: Kettle, medium sauté pan, small bowl, medium pan with tight-fitting lid, scissors

Rice

100g cashew nuts (not roasted or salted)

300g basmati rice

2 tsp mild, medium or hot curry powder (depending on how hot you like it)

100g frozen peas

Curry

2 tbsp mild, medium or hot curry powder (depending on how hot you like it)

2 tsp garam masala (easy to find in the supermarket)

1 tsp ground cinnamon

¼ tsp ground ginger

1–3 tsp medium chilli powder (depending on how hot you like it)

4 skinless, boneless chicken breasts

Vegetable oil

400ml tin of coconut milk

200ml water

1 bunch of spring onions

1 garlic clove

1 tsp caster sugar (optional)

Small handful of fresh coriander

Salt and freshly ground black pepper

I do love an Indian curry – in fact I love a curry of any description – but Sri Lankans also know how to make a good curried dish. Nestled to the southeast of southern India, just a stone's throw from the Maldives, lies a place very close to my heart, somewhere I visit often. Formerly known as Ceylon, Sri Lanka really is a feast for the senses: bright colours, vibrant flavours, wonderful beaches and people. Much of my cooking is influenced by this beautiful island, and this is my favourite Sri Lankan chicken curry.

+ Put the kettle on to boil for the rice.

+ While waiting, put a medium sauté pan on a high heat and throw in the cashew nuts (without any oil). Cook for 3–4 minutes, tossing from time to time, until golden. Tip into a small bowl and set aside. Leave the dry pan on a low heat for the curry.

+ Once the kettle has boiled, tip the rice, curry powder and a little salt into a medium pan and pour the boiled water over so it comes about 2cm above the top of the rice (this is approximately 500ml). Cover with the lid and return to the boil. Then reduce the heat to really low and cook for as long as it says on the packet. Set the timer for halfway through as you will be adding more ingredients then.

+ Now, for the curry. To the hot pan (without any oil), add the curry powder, garam masala, cinnamon, ginger and chilli powder and cook for 2–3 minutes, or until you start to really smell the spices, tossing regularly.

>

Really simple Sri Lankan chicken curry with coconut milk & cashew nut rice

(continued)

+ While they toast, snip the chicken into big bite-sized chunks with scissors and season them well with salt and pepper. Pour a good drizzle of oil into the spice pan and turn the heat up to high. Add the chicken and cook for 2–3 minutes, tossing the pieces from time to time so they brown all over.

+ By this stage the rice will be about halfway through cooking. Scatter the toasted cashew nuts and peas on top, without stirring them in, and put the lid back on for the remaining 5 minutes of cooking time.

+ Going back to the curry, remove the pan from the heat while you pour the coconut milk in along with the water. Return it to the heat, turn it up and let it bubble away for a few minutes.

+ Meanwhile, trim and finely chop the spring onions (both the green and the white bits) and peel and finely chop the garlic. Add them to the curry and leave to cook for 2–3 minutes, reducing the heat if bubbling too hard and giving it a stir from time to time.

+ Once the rice is cooked, turn off the heat, season with salt and pepper and then put the lid back on to keep the rice warm.

+ Check that the chicken is cooked by piercing with a knife – there should be no pinkness remaining. Then have a taste of the curry, adjusting the seasoning and adding the sugar if liked. Divide the rice between four plates, top with the curry, tear the coriander leaves over and serve.

Time from start to finish:
40 minutes
Serves: 4
Equipment: Large roasting tin,
2 medium bowls, zester,
colander, kettle, medium pan
with lid, grater

Chicken

1 onion

3 garlic cloves

4 large chicken legs or breasts on
the bone or 8 thigh pieces on the
bone (you can use boneless chicken
pieces also) or a mix of 16 wings and
drumsticks

3 tbsp balsamic vinegar

1–4 tbsp Tabasco sauce (as hot as you
dare!)

1 tbsp soft light brown (or caster)
sugar

2 tsp ground allspice

2 tsp English mustard powder

1 tsp ground cinnamon

A few shakes of soy sauce

1 lime

½ orange

A few fresh thyme sprigs

Pineapple salsa

½ large pineapple or 400g prepared
fresh pineapple chunks

6 cherry tomatoes

Small handful of fresh coriander

1 lime

Rice and beans

400g tin of kidney beans

Small handful of fresh coriander or flat
leaf parsley, to serve

350g easy cook long grain rice

400ml tin of coconut milk

2cm piece of fresh ginger

1 red chilli

Salt and freshly ground black pepper

Baked jerk chicken with pineapple salsa, coconut rice & beans

This may not seem like the shortest list of ingredients you have ever happened across, but upon close inspection, you'll see they are very easy to get. This recipe forms part of my Jamaican-St Lucian-Bajan-English-Polish roots. There may be some liquid left in the roasting tin after the cooking time – this is wonderful drizzled on the chicken to serve.

+ Preheat the oven to 200°C, (fan 180°C), 400°F, Gas Mark 6.

+ Peel the onion, cut it into wedges and then bash the garlic cloves open with the side of a knife. Toss them into a large roasting tin with the chicken pieces and set aside.

+ Now make up the sauce in a medium bowl. Add the balsamic vinegar, Tabasco, sugar, allspice, mustard powder, cinnamon and soy sauce. Squeeze in the juice from the lime, finely grate the zest from the orange and squeeze its juice over too. Run your fingers down the length of the thyme sprigs to release the leaves and toss them in also. Season with salt and pepper, mix together and pour half over the chicken. Toss about to coat, lay the pieces in a single layer and roast in the oven for 30 minutes.

+ Meanwhile, make the pineapple salsa. Peel, core and finely chop the pineapple, or chop the pineapple chunks into smaller cubes with a serrated knife. Quarter the cherry tomatoes and pick and roughly chop the coriander leaves. Toss them in a medium bowl with the juice from the lime, season to taste and set aside.

+ Next drain and rinse the kidney beans for the rice and pick and roughly chop the coriander or parsley leaves for the garnish, reserving both for later.

+ Put the kettle on to boil for the rice. Tip the rice into a medium pan over a high heat and add the coconut milk. Leave this to come to the boil.

>

Baked jerk chicken with pineapple salsa, coconut rice & beans

(continued)

+ Meanwhile, peel and finely grate the ginger and halve, deseed and finely chop the chilli. Once the coconut milk is boiling, add the ginger and chilli to it with enough boiled water so that all the liquid comes over the rice by about 2cm (roughly 200ml of water). Turn down the heat to low, put the lid on and cook for as long as it says on the packet. The beans need to be added 5 minutes before the rice is ready, so set your timer accordingly.

+ The chicken should be about halfway through cooking, so pour the remaining sauce over the chicken to baste.

+ When the rice has just 5 minutes left to cook, tip the kidney beans in (without stirring them in), put the lid back on and leave to finish cooking.

+ Once the cooking time is up, check the chicken is cooked by piercing it with a knife. There should be no pinkness in the meat.

+ Fluff up the now-cooked rice, gently stirring the kidney beans through, and divide between four serving plates. Sit the chicken and onion pieces on top and spoon the sauce over. Spoon the salsa beside, scatter the chopped coriander or parsley over and serve.

Sticky Asian BBQ chicken wings with sweetcorn rice & red cabbage slaw

Time from start to finish:
45 minutes
Serves: 4
Equipment: Large roasting tin, small bowl, kettle, large bowl, medium pan with lid, colander

800g mixed chicken wings and drumsticks

Sauce

6 squidges of tomato ketchup

3 tbsp balsamic vinegar

3 tbsp soy sauce

2 tbsp Chinese five-spice powder

2 squidges of honey

1 garlic clove

Few sprigs of fresh thyme

Sunflower oil

Slaw

¼ head of red cabbage

1 small red onion

1 small red chilli

1 big handful of raisins (about 25g)

Pinch of English mustard powder (optional)

2 squidges of honey

5 tbsp Greek yogurt (full fat, low fat or no fat)

1 lime

Corn rice

350g easy cook long grain rice

198g tin of sweetcorn

Sunflower oil

30g (approx) bag of fresh coriander or flat leaf parsley

Salt and freshly ground black pepper

If the weather permits, cook the chicken on the barbecue for that smoky, woody, charcoal flavour. If not, you can bake it in the oven, as I have here. Even though in my home town of London the rain has become an even more recurrent theme of late, I like to put on my rain coat and wellies and with much persistence, get that barbecue going anyway.

+ Preheat the oven to 200°C, (fan 180°C), 400°F, Gas Mark 6.

+ Scatter the chicken pieces in a large roasting tin. Put the tomato ketchup, vinegar, soy sauce, five-spice and honey in a small bowl. Peel and finely chop the garlic and run your fingers down the length of the thyme sprigs to release the leaves then add them both along with salt, pepper and a drizzle of oil. Give everything a good stir and pour it over the chicken pieces. Toss everything about to evenly coat, then settle the chicken into a single layer and put in the oven to cook for 30 minutes.

+ Next, put the kettle on to boil for the rice.

+ Meanwhile, prepare the slaw. Remove the woody core from the cabbage and then slice it up as fine as you can and put it in a large bowl. Peel and finely slice the red onion, halve, deseed and finely chop the chilli and throw these in along with the raisins, mustard powder (if using) and honey. Spoon the yogurt in, squeeze in the lime juice and season to taste with salt and pepper. Mix everything together and set aside.

+ Tip the rice into a medium pan with a little salt, pour in the now-boiled water so that it is about 2cm above the top of the rice, put the lid on and bring back to the boil. Then turn it down as low as it will go and leave to cook for as long as it says on the packet.

+ Baste the chicken with the sauce.

>

Chicken + duck mains

Sticky Asian BBQ chicken wings with sweetcorn rice & red cabbage slaw

(continued)

+ Once the rice is ready, drain it and then tip it back into the pan. Drain the sweetcorn and add it to the rice with salt, pepper and a drizzle of oil. Stir together and then put the lid on to keep warm.

+ After the chicken has been cooking for 30 minutes, check to see that it is cooked by piercing it with a knife — it should be piping hot in the middle with no pinkness. The barbecue sauce should be a sticky coating on the chicken.

+ Divide the rice between serving plates, arrange the chicken on top and spoon the slaw to the side. Rip the leaves from the coriander or parsley stalks, scatter them over and serve.

Time from start to finish:
20 minutes
Serves: 4
Equipment: Kettle, large frying
pan, sieve, medium pan with
tight-fitting lid, grater

Vegetable oil

4 skinless, boneless chicken breasts

250g basmati rice

1 tsp ground turmeric or curry powder
or pinch of saffron strands (optional)

1 bunch of spring onions

2cm piece of fresh ginger

2 garlic cloves

350ml single cream or natural yogurt
(optional; cream tastes much better but
natural yogurt is healthier)

200g tomato purée

4 tbsp garam masala

1 tbsp paprika

2 tsp English mustard powder

Fresh coriander or parsley leaves, to
serve

Salt and freshly ground black pepper

My take on chicken tikka masala with fluffy basmati rice

I love a good a chicken tikka masala. You can try to palm me off with a dansak or a korma, but a masala will always get my taste buds going. I know just how easy it is to reach for a jar of your favourite curry sauce or tikka paste, but the thing is I find making my own tikka masala so very rewarding; it literally takes only about 20 minutes to prepare and the bonus is you know exactly what is going onto your plate. The chicken can be replaced with butternut squash or lamb or beef (which will both need to be cooked for a bit less time) or fish (which will require even less time).

+ Put the kettle on to boil.

+ Drizzle some oil into a large frying pan and place on a medium to high heat. Cut the chicken breasts into bite-sized chunks and fry for 5 minutes, tossing from time to time, until brown all over.

+ Tip the rice into a medium pan and add the turmeric (or curry powder or saffron strands), if using. Pour over enough boiled water to come about 2cm above the rice (roughly 500ml of water, to be pedantic).

+ Cover with the lid and return to the boil. Then reduce the heat to low and leave to cook for as long as it says on the packet.

+ While that is cooking away, give the chicken a little toss and then trim and finely slice the spring onions (both the green and the white bits), peel and grate the ginger and peel and finely chop the garlic.

>

Tandoori chicken wraps with cucumber raita & mango salsa

(continued)

+ Now prepare the mango salsa. If using a whole mango, slice the two cheeks off either side of the stone. Cut them in half, run the knife through the flesh close to the skin to peel it, then dice the flesh into bite-sized pieces. If you are using ready-prepared mango, cut it into small cubes. Pick and finely chop the coriander leaves and toss these and the mango into a medium bowl. Squeeze the lime juice over, season with salt and pepper to taste, then spoon into a small serving bowl and set aside.

+ Take the tortillas from the oven, remove from the foil and place the stack on a serving plate. Check your chicken is cooked. There should be no pinkness and it should be piping hot in the centre. Spoon into a serving bowl for sharing with the raita and mango salsa alongside.

Scrumptious spicy chicken fajitas with guacamole, salsa & sour cream

Time from start to finish:
30 minutes
Serves: 4
Equipment: Small bowl, 2 medium bowls, baking sheet, large sauté pan or wok

Accompaniments

Small handful of fresh chives

200g sour cream

Small handful of fresh coriander

1 red chilli (optional)

1 lime

200g cherry tomatoes

1 tsp caster sugar (optional)

2 ripe avocados

1 spring onion

Fajitas

1 garlic clove

1 red onion

1 red pepper

1 orange pepper

8 corn or wheat tortillas

Spicy chicken·

Olive oil

4 medium skinless, boneless chicken breasts

1 tbsp paprika

2 tsp ground cumin

1 tsp dried oregano

1 lime

Salt and freshly ground black pepper

If you are like me, there have been many times when you may have reached for the packet of fajitas with that sachet that you just tip in. I do know how scrummy they can be, truly, but once I made my own, I never looked back. Change things up each time you make it — strips of frying beef or prawns are a sound alternative.

+ Firstly, prepare the accompaniments. Finely chop the chives, place in a small bowl with the sour cream and stir together.

+ Then, for the salsa and guacamole. Rip the leaves off the coriander, roughly chop them and divide between two medium bowls. Then deseed and finely chop the chilli, if using, and again, divide between the bowls. Cut the lime in half and squeeze half into each bowl also.

+ Quarter the cherry tomatoes and add to one of the bowls. Stir to combine and then season to taste with salt and pepper, also adding the sugar if you think it needs it.

+ Then to finish the guacamole, halve the avocados, discard their stones, scoop the flesh into the other bowl and give it a little mash with a fork. Trim and finely slice the spring onion (both the green and the white bits) and add also, giving everything a good mix together and season to taste.

+ Preheat the oven to 180°C, (fan 160°C), 350°F, Gas Mark 4.

+ Next prepare the fajita mixture. Peel and finely chop the garlic, peel and finely slice the red onion, halve and deseed the peppers and then cut each into thin strips and set aside.

+ Remove the tortillas from the packet and place the stack on a sheet of tin foil. Wrap them up tightly, sit the parcel on a baking sheet and place in the oven for 10–15 minutes to warm through.

>

Scrumptious spicy chicken fajitas with guacamole, salsa & sour cream

(continued)

+ Meanwhile, cook the chicken. Put a good drizzle of oil in a large sauté pan or wok over a high heat. While the oil heats up, cut the chicken into short, thin strips and then carefully add them to the hot oil. Cook for 2–3 minutes, stirring from time to time, until they start turning golden brown.

+ Add the paprika, cumin and oregano and season well with salt and pepper. Halve the lime and squeeze in the juice and then add the reserved garlic, red onion and peppers.

+ Reduce the heat to medium and keep everything cooking for another 6–8 minutes or until the chicken is piping hot and cooked through with no pinkness and the peppers are just beginning to soften, then remove from the heat.

+ Spoon the accompaniments into serving bowls. Remove the tortillas from the oven, carefully unwrap and stack on a serving plate.

+ Spoon the cooked chicken mixture into a serving bowl. My family like this served with everything in the middle of the table. Then it is a big free-for-all as everyone dives in!

Time from start to finish:
35 minutes
Serves: 4
Equipment: Large sauté pan,
scissors, kettle, large pan with
lid, colander

Vegetable oil

4 rashers of bacon

4 skinless, boneless chicken breasts or
8 skinless, boneless chicken thighs

1 bunch of spring onions

150g chestnut mushrooms

2 garlic cloves

2 sprigs of fresh rosemary

2 x 400g tins of chopped tomatoes

A good glug (about 100ml) of
Madeira (or red or white wine or
chicken stock)

3 tbsp tomato purée or 1 tbsp harissa
paste (you can get it from most
supermarkets)

Pinch of dried oregano

1 dried bay leaf

300g of your favourite pasta (I love to
use penne or rigatoni)

1–2 tsp caster sugar (optional)

Knob of butter (optional)

Small handful of fresh basil or parsley
leaves (optional)

Salt and freshly ground black pepper

Chicken cacciatore with harissa, bacon & rosemary

Recently, I have become a bit of a chicken thigh person, finding the meat moister and more succulent than the ubiquitous chicken breast. The addition of harissa, the spicy, tomatoey Moroccan paste, adds a subtle kick to this 'hunter-style' Italian dish, but for those not in love with an extra bit of spice, then tomato purée works beautifully too.

+ Put a drizzle of oil into a large sauté pan on a high heat. Use scissors to snip the bacon rashers into bite-sized pieces. Add them to the pan once hot and fry for a couple of minutes, stirring every so often, until they are browned.

+ While this cooks, season the chicken pieces well with salt and pepper.

+ Remove the bacon from the pan, leaving the fat behind, and set aside to drain on some kitchen paper. Put the chicken in, top side down, reduce the heat to medium and leave to cook for about 4 minutes.

+ Meanwhile, trim and finely slice the spring onions (both the green and the white bits) and mushrooms and peel and finely chop the garlic. Run your fingers down the length of the rosemary stalks to release their leaves and finely chop them too. Set everything aside.

+ The chicken pieces should now be golden brown underneath, so flip them over and leave to cook on the other side for about 3 minutes.

+ Once the chicken is golden brown, turn down the heat to low and add the prepared mushrooms, garlic and rosemary, along with the tomatoes, Madeira (or red or white wine or stock), tomato purée or harissa paste and oregano, and crumble in the bay leaf.

+ Give it a good stir and then leave to bubble away for 15–20 minutes, stirring from time to time so that it does not catch on the bottom.

>

Chicken cacciatore with harissa, bacon & rosemary

(continued)

+ When the chicken dish is about halfway through cooking, add the reserved cooked bacon and spring onions, then put the kettle on. Use the boiled water to cook the pasta in a large pan according to the packet's instructions. Once it is cooked, drain the pasta and then return it to the pan with the lid on to keep warm if necessary.

+ Check to see if the chicken is cooked — if the juices run clear, it is ready. Taste the sauce, adding a little sugar and/or a knob of butter if the sauce is still a bit acidic from the tomatoes. Add a drizzle of water if the sauce is too thick and let it bubble away for a bit more if too thin.

+ Divide the pasta between four plates, top with a piece of chicken, spoon some sauce over and scatter with some ripped-up basil or parsley leaves, if using.

Time from start to finish:
35 minutes
Serves: 4
Equipment: Large roasting tin,
peeler, large sauté or casserole
pan with tight-fitting lid,
large plate

750g baby or new potatoes

3 large carrots

Vegetable oil

1 tbsp fennel seeds

8 chicken thighs, skin on and bone in

12 cocktail sausages or 4 regular sausages

2 sprigs of fresh rosemary

A few sprigs of fresh sage

2 garlic cloves

1 bunch of spring onions

2 Granny Smith apples

4 tsp plain flour

500ml cider (or chicken stock)

Salt and freshly ground black pepper

Chicken, apple & cider casserole with fennel seed roasted veg

I made this dish with regular sausages, but once the dish was ready, each sausage had shot right out of its jacket. Not a problem for most – in fact they are just the ticket to provide some cheap humour at the dinner table – but this problem can easily be solved by carefully removing the skins from the sausages before adding them to the casserole with the chicken.

+ Preheat the oven to 220°C, (fan 200°C), 425°F, Gas Mark 7.

+ Slice the potatoes into 5mm slices and scatter them into a large roasting tin. Peel and slice the carrots into 1cm pieces and scatter them over. Season everything well with salt and pepper and drizzle with oil. Scatter the fennel seeds over, toss gently together and lay everything out in as even a layer as possible. Place in the oven to roast for 30 minutes.

+ Next put some oil in a large sauté or casserole pan over a high heat. While this heats up, season the chicken with a good amount of salt and pepper and then put half of the chicken in the pan, skin side down. Nestle half of the sausages around the chicken and fry for 4 minutes. Don't move the chicken but turn the sausages every so often to give them a nice golden colour all over.

+ Meanwhile, run your fingers down the length of the rosemary sprigs to release the leaves, pick the sage leaves and then set them aside.

+ Once the chicken skin is crisp and golden brown, flip the pieces over and let the 'meaty' side cook for 1 minute. Then remove the chicken and sausages from the pan and place on a large plate. Repeat with the remaining chicken and sausages.

+ Peel and finely slice the garlic and then trim and chop the spring onions (both the green and the white bits) into 1cm pieces. Quarter the apples,

>

Five-spice roasted duck breast with cherry & Shiraz sauce & sesame noodles

(continued)

+ Check the duck breasts. When cooked they should be piping hot in the middle. I test mine by inserting a skewer into the centre and leaving it for a moment, then pulling it out and carefully testing the temperature on my hand.

+ Remove the cooked duck breasts onto a plate, then cover loosely with tin foil to rest for a few minutes. This will make the flesh much more juicy.

+ By now, the sauce should be thickened and syrupy. Season with salt and pepper to taste.

+ Finally, once the noodles are cooked season them to taste and then divide them between four plates and top each with a duck breast. Drizzle the sauce over, rip over some coriander leaves, if you fancy, and serve.

Beef, lamb + pork mains

'Observe the masses and do the opposite.'
Walt Disney

It has only been in recent years that I have really got into beef, lamb and pork. And my goodness, have I got into it. I suppose before I became a chef, I was not really sure what to do with these three majestic meats. But then I started buying different cuts and types and began experimenting, messing around with flavours and colours and textures. I believe that a lot of the time, unless you can spend a hefty sum on meat (or have the luxury of a butcher right on your doorstep), it does not taste so good. However, with a little bit of help from various spice rack staples, handsome herbs and other easy ingredients, these familiar meats can be turned into something really special for a quick and easy meal.

Time from start to finish:
35 minutes
Serves: **4**
Equipment: **Large baking tray, large bowl, large frying pan, plate, baking tray**

Potato wedges

4 large floury baking potatoes

8 garlic cloves

Olive oil

Burgers

½ bunch of spring onions

1 garlic clove

500g lean minced beef

50g dried natural breadcrumbs

Big dollop (about 1 tbsp) of American mustard

A couple of squidges (about 1 tbsp) of tomato ketchup

A few shakes of Worcestershire sauce

1 medium egg

2 sprigs of fresh thyme

Olive oil

Salt and freshly ground black pepper

To serve

1 large tomato

100g Cheddar or blue cheese

1 small red onion

4 burger buns (I like mine with a sesame seed top)

A little butter (optional)

A few dollops of yellow mustard

1 bag of wild rocket

Extra virgin olive oil

Balsamic vinegar

Ketchup or HP sauce (optional)

Good old-fashioned burger with rocket, red onions (plus all the trimmings) & garlicky potato wedges

I tested these over and over again to get the flavours just right. A squidge of this there and a dollop of that here and I think I have got it just right. They really go down a storm at home.

+ Preheat the oven to 220°C, (fan 200°C), 425°F, Gas Mark 7.

+ Cut each potato in half lengthways and then cut each piece into four or five long wedges. Peel the garlic and slam it with the side of a knife to slightly crush. Toss both onto a large baking tray, drizzle a good amount of oil over and season with salt and pepper. Toss everything together and then even out into a single layer. Roast in the oven for 30 minutes.

+ Meanwhile, trim and really finely slice the spring onions (both the green and white bits), peel and finely chop the garlic and add both to a large bowl. Tip in the minced beef, add the breadcrumbs, American mustard, tomato ketchup and Worcestershire sauce and crack in the egg.

+ Slide your thumb and forefinger down the thyme sprigs to remove the leaves in one go and add those to the bowl with a good amount of salt and pepper.

+ Before you get your hands into the mixture, put a good drizzle of oil in a large frying pan on a high heat. Then back to the mixture and squidge it together with your hands until everything is well combined. Divide into four equal-sized pieces, shape each into a 2.5cm thick patty and place on a plate.

+ Carefully add the burgers to the pan, reduce the heat to medium and leave to fry on the first side for 5–6 minutes.

+ As these cook, slice up the tomato and cheese (or crumble the blue cheese if using). Peel and finely slice the onion.

>

Rich rump steak 'sort-of-stew' with port, porcini & herby dumplings

(continued)

+ Meanwhile, finely slice up the spring onions (the green and white bits), peel and roughly chop the garlic and roughly chop the sage and add to the cooked lardons. Cut the butternut squash and sweet potato pieces in half if large and then add to the pan and sweat for 2–3 minutes.

+ Roughly chop the sundried tomatoes and add to the pan along with 3 tablespoons of the flour, the dried porcini mushrooms, jam to sweeten (if using), bay leaf and Worcestershire sauce. Stir together before adding the beef stock and port (if using). Whack up the heat and let it boil away to reduce for about 10 minutes or so until thickened.

+ While this is bubbling away, put a medium frying pan on a low heat with a good drizzle of oil. While the oil is heating up, trim the rump steak of excess fat, cut into big bite-sized chunks and put in a medium bowl. Add the remaining tablespoon of flour, the mustard powder and a good amount of salt and pepper and then toss everything together so the meat is well coated.

+ Turn the heat up to high under the frying pan and carefully add about half of the meat. Brown it well all over for about 2–3 minutes before tipping onto a plate and repeating with the next batch. Doing it in small batches like this means the meat will brown nicely rather than stew in its juices, which adds to the flavour.

+ Season the sauce with salt and pepper to taste and carefully tip the meat and any juices in. Spoon a little of the sauce into the meat-searing pan and simmer on a low heat for a minute or two, scraping any sticky bits from the bottom. Tip this back into the stew for extra flavour, reduce the heat and leave to simmer away very gently for about another 10 minutes until the meat and vegetables are tender and the sauce thickened and rich.

+ Remove the dumplings from the oven. They should be crusty and golden on the outside and cooked through.

+ Then to serve, I either take it straight to the table in the casserole pot with the dumplings nestled on top or divide the stew between four plates, arranging a few dumplings on each one. Either way, roughly chop the parsley (if using) and scatter over to serve.

Prep time: **25 minutes**
Time baking in the oven:
25 minutes
Serves: **4**
Equipment: **Large pan, peeler, sieve set over a small bowl, kettle, medium pan, grater, small pan (or bowl and microwave), 20cm-square baking dish at least 5cm deep (about 2 litres), medium bowl**

Pie filling

Vegetable oil

2 sprigs of fresh rosemary

4 fresh sage leaves

750g lamb mince

3 carrots

1 spring onion

1 garlic clove

400g tin of chopped tomatoes

2 tbsp plain flour

400ml beef stock (or a good red wine or Madeira)

100g tomato purée

2 tbsp Worcestershire sauce

1 handful (about 25g) of dried porcini mushrooms (optional)

50g Cheddar cheese (optional)

1 tsp caster sugar

100g frozen peas

Rosti

1 medium potato

1 medium sweet potato

25g butter

Whole nutmeg (optional)

Salad

4 tbsp extra virgin olive oil

2 tbsp balsamic vinegar

1 tsp Dijon mustard

2 bags of wild rocket or mixed leaves

Salt and freshly ground black pepper

Rosemary roast cottage pie with a crispy rosti topping

Not a pint-sized list of ingredients, I agree, but family demands for inclusion of a cottage pie had to be met. The crispy rosti topping adds some welcome crunch to this classic British dish.

+ Preheat the oven to 200°C, (fan 180°C), 400°F, Gas Mark 6.

+ Place a large pan, with a good drizzle of oil, on a high heat for the cottage pie filling. Run your fingers down the length of the rosemary to release the leaves and then roughly chop them along with the sage. Add to the pan with the lamb mince and leave to cook for 4–5 minutes or until the meat is browned all over, stirring occasionally.

+ While that is cooking away, peel the carrots and cut them into small dice and peel and finely chop the garlic. Stir them into the browned meat and cook for a further minute or two. Finely chop the spring onion (both the green and white bits) and set aside.

+ Meanwhile, drain the tin of tomatoes through a sieve set over a small bowl to catch the juices. Then stir the flour into the meat mixture really well before adding the tomatoes from the sieve. (You are not using the juices in this recipe but they can be frozen for later use in a soup or stew for example.)

+ Add the stock (or red wine or Madeira), tomato purée, Worcestershire sauce and porcini mushrooms (if using) and stir a couple of times before leaving it to bubble away for about 15 minutes.

+ In the meantime, prepare the rosti topping. Put the kettle on. Peel the potatoes, cut the normal one in half (leaving the sweet potato whole) and place them into a medium pan with a little salt. Cover them with the boiled water and return to the boil on a high heat, before reducing it to simmer for about 5 minutes.

+ While they are cooking, you can roughly grate the cheese (if using) and set it aside for the topping. Melt the butter for the rosti in a small pan (or bowl in the microwave) and set aside also.

>

Rosemary roast cottage pie with a crispy rosti topping

(continued)

+ When the potatoes have been cooking for about 5 minutes, drain them really well and set them aside for a few minutes or until cool enough to handle.

+ Roughly grate the potatoes, toss them together gently on a board and season them really well with salt and pepper.

+ Remove the sauce from the heat, add the spring onions and season to taste with salt and pepper. I also like to add a little sugar to soften the sharpness of the tomatoes. Stir the frozen peas in and tip the whole thing into the baking dish.

+ Scatter the potato mix over the pie, fluffing it up a bit with a fork, then gently brush the melted butter over the top. Grate over some nutmeg, if using, and bake in the oven for 25 minutes.

+ Scatter the cheese over 5 minutes before the end of the cooking time. Then mix the oil, balsamic vinegar, Dijon mustard and some salt and pepper together in a medium bowl. Toss the rocket or mixed leaves through to dress.

+ Once cooked, the potato should be tender all the way through, crispy on top and just catching colour. Remove the cottage pie from the oven and serve straight to the table with the bowl of dressed leaves.

Time from start to finish:
30 minutes
Serves: **4**
Equipment: **Kettle, large sauté pan (preferably not non-stick), scissors, medium pan with tight-fitting lid, plate**

Sunflower oil

2 sirloin steaks (about 225g each)

300g Thai jasmine rice

1 red pepper

1 aubergine

2 garlic cloves

4cm piece of fresh ginger

6 tbsp Thai red curry paste

2 x 400ml tins of coconut milk

3 tbsp fish sauce

1 bunch of spring onions

1 handful of seedless red grapes (about 50g) (optional)

1 small handful of fresh basil leaves, to serve

Salt and freshly ground black pepper

Thai red beef curry with jasmine rice

Last year the family went to Thailand as a Christmas treat. We stayed in the most beautiful hotel with views over the vibrant aquamarine sea. Every day I would order the same thing for dinner: the red beef curry. The heat of the ginger, the creaminess of the coconut milk and the sweetness of the red grapes made for a multi-layered taste extravaganza that I just had to recreate at home. The beef can be replaced by chicken or even butternut squash for a simple variation.

+ Put the kettle on to boil and put a large sauté pan on a medium to high heat with a drizzle of oil in.

+ Meanwhile, cut the fat off the side of the steak (I find the easiest way to do this is with scissors). Season the steaks really well with a good amount of salt and pepper and then lower them into the hot fat and leave to cook for about 3 minutes.

+ Meanwhile, tip the rice into a medium pan. Pour over enough boiled water to come about 2cm above the rice (roughly 500ml of water, to be pedantic). Cover with the lid and return to the boil. Then reduce the heat to low and leave to cook for as long as it says on the packet.

+ Next halve and deseed the pepper, then cut it into big bite-sized chunks and set aside.

+ Flip the steaks over to the other side and cook for another 3 minutes.

+ Continue to prepare the vegetables. Trim and cut the aubergine into big bite-sized pieces, peel and finely chop the garlic and peel and slice the ginger into sticks.

+ Remove the steaks from the pan (leaving the pan on the heat) and leave to rest on a plate covered with tin foil.

>

Thai red beef curry
with jasmine rice

(continued)

+ Pour 1 tablespoon of water into the pan and scrape up any tasty bits left from the steak. Stir in the curry paste and allow to cook for 30 seconds. Then add the red pepper, aubergine, garlic and ginger. Stir well together to combine and pour in the coconut milk and fish sauce. Turn up the heat, bring to the boil and then reduce the heat a little and leave it to bubble away gently for 8 minutes.

+ Check the rice is now tender and, if so, remove from the heat, fluff up with a fork and cover with the lid to keep warm.

+ Next slice up the spring onions and halve the grapes (if using) and set them aside.

+ Slice up the rested beef into 5mm slithers. Then add them to the curry along with the resting juices, spring onions and grapes (if using). Season to taste with salt and pepper and a little more fish sauce, if liked, and then cook for another minute or so.

+ Divide the rice between four plates and top with the curry. Sprinkle over the basil and serve.

Prep time: 30 minutes
Time baking in the oven:
20 minutes
Serves: 6
Equipment: Kettle, 25.5cm-
square baking dish about 6cm
deep (2.5 litres), baking tray,
small pan with lid, large pan,
2 medium bowls, colander,
grater, mug or small bowl

3 medium potatoes

Vegetable oil

600g minced lamb (or beef)

1 bunch of spring onions

2 garlic cloves

2 tbsp plain flour

400g tin of chopped tomatoes (the
ones with the herbs in are nice but not
essential)

1 glass of a good red wine (or
Marsala or beef or chicken stock)

6 tbsp Worcestershire sauce

4 tbsp tomato purée

1 tbsp ground cumin

3 tsp ground cinnamon

3 tsp dried oregano

2 sprigs of fresh thyme

1 large aubergine

Olive oil

Small handful of fresh mint, to serve

White sauce

125g Parmesan cheese

250g tub of ricotta cheese

2 medium egg yolks

A pinch of freshly grated nutmeg

Salad

6 tbsp extra virgin olive oil

3 tbsp red wine vinegar

1 bag of watercress leaves

Salt and freshly ground black pepper

The mighty moussaka

I squeezed this dish into the book as it is faster than most moussakas. I know it may not be the most pure of moussaka recipes, but for my family it is one that both satisfies the tummy and pleases the palate. All the sauce ingredients go straight in the pan and I have also come up with a simple 'white sauce', which can be made in a matter of seconds and is rich and creamy and incredibly flavoursome.

+ Preheat the oven to 220°C, (fan 200°C), 425°F, Gas Mark 7 and put the kettle on to boil for the potatoes. Sit the baking dish on a baking tray and set aside.

+ Wash the potatoes well and then slice them up into 1cm-thick rounds. Place in a small pan with a pinch of salt and pour the now-boiled water over. Put on a high heat with the lid on to bring the water back to the boil quickly.

+ Meanwhile, put a drizzle of oil in a large pan over a really high heat. Fry half of the lamb (or beef) mince for a few minutes, stirring regularly, until it all gets nice and coloured. Tip it into a medium bowl while you brown the remaining meat.

+ Once the potato pan is boiling away, remove the lid and leave to cook for about 8 minutes.

+ Next, slice up the spring onions (both the green and white bits) and peel and slice the garlic.

+ Return all the mince to the pan and stir in the flour. Then add the spring onions, garlic, tinned tomatoes, red wine (or Marsala or beef or chicken stock), Worcestershire sauce, tomato purée, cumin, cinnamon and oregano. Run your fingers down the length of the thyme sprigs to release their leaves and add them with some salt and pepper. Stir well and cook on a low heat for 5 minutes. Give it a stir from time to time so it does not catch on the bottom.

>

Maple and balsamic-glazed lamb chops with mint, toasted almonds & feta cous cous

(continued)

+ Check the cous cous grains have absorbed all the water and are tender and then fluff it up with a fork. Crumble the feta cheese in, season with salt and pepper and add a good drizzle of oil. Stir together and re-cover to keep warm.

+ The glaze should be thickened and syrupy (a little bit thinner than golden syrup), so remove from the heat and keep warm.

+ Cut into the centre of one of the lamb chops or cutlets to check that they are cooked to your liking. When ready, remove them onto a large plate to rest for a few minutes, covered with tin foil (this will make them much more tender and juicy).

+ Add the spring onions and flaked almonds to the frying pan and cook on a medium heat for 1–2 minutes, stirring them a bit every now and then. Remove from the heat when the spring onions are wilted and the almonds golden.

+ Divide the cous cous between four serving plates. Sit the rested lamb chops on top and drizzle the glaze (and any resting juices) over. Scatter over the onion and almond mix and rip up the mint leaves. If using, top with the pomegranate seeds and serve.

Lozza's lamb biryani

Time from start to finish:
25 minutes
Serves: **4**
Equipment: **Medium pan with tight-fitting lid, sieve**

Vegetable oil

5 cardamom pods

2 tsp garam masala

2 tsp ground turmeric

1 tsp ground cumin

1 tsp hot or medium chilli powder (or more if you want a bit of extra heat)

1 bunch of spring onions

500g lamb chump steaks

350g basmati rice

400ml tin of coconut milk

100ml water

100g sundried tomatoes

Small handful of fresh coriander or mint

50g raisins

Knob of butter (optional)

25g toasted flaked almonds (they come ready toasted from the supermarket)

Salt and freshly ground black pepper

My close friends call me Lozza, so I could not resist using my nickname for alliteration for the name of this recipe! This also works really well with chicken, beef or prawns instead of the lamb. Now it is not strictly a traditional recipe, but it is packed full of wonderful flavours and is a pretty good imitation. I believe that traditionally this Moghul dish is flavoured with saffron which I have left out, but feel free to add a stamen or two to the rice if you fancy it.

+ Put a drizzle of oil in a medium pan on a low heat. Slam the cardamom pods open with the side of a knife and add to the pan with the garam masala, turmeric, cumin and chilli powder and cook for 3–4 minutes, stirring occasionally.

+ While this cooks, trim and finely slice the spring onions (both the green and the white bits) and then chop the lamb up into bite-sized cubes. Turn the pan heat up to high, add a little more oil and add the spring onions and lamb. Brown the meat all over for 2–3 minutes, stirring often so nothing catches on the bottom.

+ Then add the rice to the pan with the coconut milk and 100ml of water.

+ Cover with a tight-fitting lid, bring to the boil and then turn it down to a very gentle simmer and leave to cook away for as long as the rice says on the packet (usually 10–12 minutes). Don't be tempted to stir the rice.

+ Meanwhile, roughly chop up the sundried tomatoes and the coriander or mint and set aside.

+ Once the rice is cooked, stir in the sundried tomatoes, half the coriander or mint and the raisins. Let them heat through for a moment or two.

+ Taste the rice, adding any salt and pepper if it needs it and even a knob of butter to make it extra creamy, if you like. Then serve with a scattering of the remaining chopped herbs over the top along with the toasted flaked almonds, if using.

Prep time: **10 minutes**
Time baking in the oven: **4 hours**
Serves: **4**
Equipment: **Casserole pot (big enough to fit the lamb) with lid, roasting tin**

½ leg of lamb (the thick fillet end), with bone in (about 1kg)

2 red onions

8 garlic cloves

4 sprigs of fresh rosemary

4 fresh sage leaves

2 bay leaves

400ml white wine (any wine will do)

A couple of squidges of honey

1kg roasting potatoes

Olive oil

300g frozen peas

Salt and freshly ground black pepper

Slow-roast, fast-prep leg of lamb with Aussie Chardonnay, rosemary, sage & bay

Now, this is a slow-cook but very fast-prep dish, so I thought I would add it to the book. I made this at home one Sunday. I literally just lobbed all the ingredients in the pot and then left it to cook for ages. I seriously was not expecting anything amazing; just, I thought, a bit of lamb for dinner. But when it was cooked, I tasted a little while it was still on the kitchen counter and I almost ate the whole darn lot and did that little dance people sometimes do when something tastes really good. When I took it to the kitchen table to my hungry family, basically half eaten, they were, to say the least, not amused. I ended up slinging some chops on the grill to make up for it. (Methinks I am perhaps revealing too much here!) I am not ashamed to admit I love a good Aussie Chard and the powerful flavours work well in this dish. Having said that, any white wine will be great to cook with too.

+ Remove the lamb from the fridge 30 minutes before cooking (to bring it to room temperature) if you have time. Preheat the oven to 150°C, (fan 130°C), 300°F, Gas Mark 2, and make sure the shelves are set to fit the casserole pot and roasting tin.

+ Place the lamb in the casserole pot and season it really well with salt and pepper. Cut the onions into quarters, keeping the roots intact, peel off the skin and throw them in along with the (unpeeled) garlic cloves, rosemary sprigs, sage and bay leaves. Pour in the white wine and drizzle the

>

Sweet & sour pork balls with crunchy peanut rice

(continued)

+ While this cooks, tip the peanuts into a pestle and mortar (or use a mug and the end of a rolling pin) and bash them up a bit. Trim and slice the spring onions (the green and white bits) and reserve for serving.

+ Check that the rice is ready, add a knob of butter, salt and pepper and the nuts. Stir and cover with the lid to keep warm.

+ Check that the pork balls are piping hot and cooked through by now, and the sauce slightly reduced and thickened, then it's time to serve.

+ Divide the crunchy peanut rice between four plates and top with the pork balls and sauce. Scatter over the spring onions and eat!

Time from start to finish:
25 minutes
Serves: **4**
Equipment: **Kettle, large pan and lid, large frying pan, plate, colander**

Champ

1kg floury potatoes

1 bunch of spring onions

50g butter

Pork steaks

Vegetable oil

3 sprigs of fresh tarragon

4–8 pork loin steaks (depending on size)

Sauce

3 shallots

300g chestnut mushrooms

2 garlic cloves

25g butter

100ml white wine (or Calvados or chicken stock)

250ml cream

1 tbsp Dijon mustard

Salt and freshly ground black pepper

Tasty tarragon pork steaks with creamy mustard mushroom sauce & spring onion champ

I don't buy pork steaks that often, but when I need a quick-fix dinner they are always what seem to be left on the meat shelves of my corner store. So to make them into something special, some tarragon and a creamy mushroom sauce are most definitely the order of the day. This champ, for my family, is a winner and makes the usual mash into something really special.

+ Put the kettle on. While you wait, peel the potatoes and cut them into about 2cm-thick slices. Tip them into a large pan set on a high heat. Pour the boiled water over, pop the lid on and when it comes back to the boil, remove the lid and leave to bubble away for 10–12 minutes or until tender.

+ Meanwhile, cook the pork. Put a good drizzle of oil into a large frying pan over a medium to high heat. Pick the leaves from the tarragon and finely chop them. Season the pork steaks on both sides and then rub the tarragon in with your hands. Add the pork steaks to the pan and leave to fry for about 4 minutes on their first side.

+ While they are cooking away, start preparing the sauce ingredients by peeling and finely chopping the shallots. After the pork has been cooking for 4 minutes, flip it over to cook for another 4 minutes. Then finely slice the mushrooms and peel and finely chop the garlic for the sauce. Trim and finely slice the spring onions (the green and white bits) for the champ.

+ The pork steaks should now be cooked. They should have no pinkness remaining in their centre and be lovely and golden on the outside. Remove them onto a plate and cover with tin foil to rest and keep warm.

>

Pan-fried pork chop with a watercress, peach & Stilton salad & a lemon ginger dressing

(continued)

+ Meanwhile, prepare the dressing. Grate the ginger (skin and all) into a mug or small bowl. Squeeze in the juice of the lemon, add the oil, mustard powder (if using), a squidge of honey and some salt and pepper. Whisk well with a fork and put to the side.

+ When the pork has finished cooking, check to see that the chops are piping hot in centre with no pinkness. Then just turn off the heat and let them sit for a couple of minutes in the pan.

+ Finally, pour the dressing over the salad. Then, arrange the pork chops on the other end of the platter and serve to the table for sharing.

Time from start to finish:
25 minutes
Serves: **4**
Equipment: **Medium sauté
pan, kettle, large pan with lid,
colander**

Olive oil

2 garlic cloves

150g cubed pancetta (the one with
herbs added already is nice if you
can find it)

1 red chilli

2 x 400g tins of cherry tomatoes
(tinned chopped tomatoes will
work well also)

1 small glass of red wine

3 squidges of tomato purée

2 tsp paprika

2 tsp dried oregano

2 sprigs of fresh thyme

350g penne pasta

Extra virgin olive oil

1–2 tsp caster sugar (optional)

Salt and freshly ground black pepper

To serve

1 bunch of fresh basil

50g Parmesan cheese

Dad's penne all'arrabbiata with crispy pancetta & basil

On one of my weekend trips to my dad's house, way back in my youth, he served up a steaming hot bowl of pasta. When I asked him what it was, he said it was 'pasta with a hot, angry sauce' — the very tasty penne all'arrabbiata. I love eating at my dad's. His cooking is Italian, warm and welcoming, so it is a pleasure to be able to share this recipe with you.

+ Put a small drizzle of olive oil into a medium sauté pan on a medium heat. Peel and finely chop the garlic while you wait. Once the oil is hot, tip in the pancetta and let it cook away for a few minutes, stirring it from time to time, until it is crisp and golden brown all over. Then add the garlic and cook for 1 minute more, being careful that it doesn't burn.

+ Chop up the chilli, leaving the seeds in if you like it very hot. Throw it into the pan along with the tinned tomatoes, red wine, tomato purée, paprika and oregano. Pick the leaves from the thyme and add them with some salt and pepper then leave everything to bubble away for about 15 minutes. Stir the sauce now and again so that it does not catch on the bottom.

+ While this cooks, put the kettle on to boil for the pasta. Put a large pan on the hob, pour in the boiling water, tip in the pasta and cook according to the packet instructions.

+ Once the pasta is cooked, drain it well and then return it to the pan it was cooked in. Drizzle with some extra virgin olive oil, season with salt and pepper and put the lid on to keep it warm while you finish the sauce.

+ The sauce should now be lovely and rich and thick. Remove it from the heat and give it a taste. If the tomatoes are still tasting a bit acidic, add a teaspoon or two of caster sugar and return it to the heat for a moment or so. Then taste again, adding a little salt and pepper if you feel it needs it.

+ Tip the pasta into the sauce, mix well and then divide between four bowls. I am told that parsley is the traditional herb to top this dish, but I love some ripped-up basil and a little freshly grated Parmesan to finish.

Fish + shellfish mains

'Smooth seas do not make a skilful mariner.'
African proverb

I have always been a fish lover. Since that first bite of a fishfinger covered in bright orange breadcrumbs I knew that fish and I were going to have a long and happy relationship. It is a shame that so much of our waters are being over-fished, and not to harp on about the issue, but I always try to buy fish with the MSC stamp on it wherever possible to ensure that it is sustainably caught and not depleting our stocks. Salmon makes several appearances in this chapter. Its oily flesh goes well with so many things and it is also big enough to stand on its own two feet, with little needed for added flavour. White fish fillets, which often need a bit of a guiding hand to add tang, bite and piquancy to boost their delicate taste, are also out in force, along with their other fish partners in crime, such as tuna and trout.

Time from start to finish:
25 minutes
Serves: 2
Equipment: Blender or food
processor, 2 baking trays, large
bowl, mug

2 chunky sustainably caught skinless
cod fillets
Salt and freshly ground black pepper

Tapenade

50g pitted black olives
2 tbsp extra virgin olive oil
1 tbsp capers
1 small sprig of fresh rosemary
1 small garlic clove

Salad

½ ciabatta loaf
A drizzle of extra virgin olive oil
125g cherry tomatoes
½ cucumber
1 red onion
30g bag of fresh basil

Dressing

4 tbsp extra virgin olive oil
2 tbsp sherry vinegar
Pinch of sugar (optional)

Tapenade-crusted cod on a bed of crunchy ciabatta, tomato & basil

The Italian side of my family may not look at me with delight as I change the traditional panzanella, which is usually soaked until soggy, to crispy, crunchy croutons that require a noisy eat. Sounds obvious, but I always buy the best extra virgin olive oil I can afford and hide it far away from the family, to be brought out only for dressings and drizzling over sublime dishes such as this.

+ Preheat the oven to 200°C, (fan 180°C), 400°F, Gas Mark 6.

+ To make the tapenade, place the olives, oil and capers in a blender or food processor. Run your fingers along the rosemary stalk to remove the leaves, peel the garlic and pop both in. Season with a little salt (remembering the olives are salty) and pepper and blitz until fairly smooth.

+ Place the fish fillets on a baking tray and smear the tapenade over the top. Put in the oven for 10–12 minutes.

+ Then start the salad. Tear the bread into bite-sized chunks and toss on a baking tray with a drizzle of oil. Bake in the oven for 6–8 minutes.

+ Meanwhile, cut the cherry tomatoes in half, slice up the cucumber and throw both into a large bowl. Peel and finely slice the onion, pull the basil leaves from their stalks and add both ingredients.

+ Next make the dressing in a mug. Pour the oil in along with the sherry vinegar and sugar, if using. Season with salt and pepper to taste and whisk the mixture up a little with a fork.

+ Remove the bread from the oven once crisp and golden. Throw it in with the salad, drizzle with the dressing and toss everything together.

+ Check the fish is cooked; it should be opaque and piping hot all the way through to the centre. Once ready, remove it from the oven.

+ Divide the salad between two serving plates. Top with the cod and serve. This ciabatta salad for me is so addictive!

Time from start to finish:
35 minutes
Serves: 4
Equipment: Large baking tray,
food processor, large bowl,
grater, large frying pan, plate,
baking tray

Baked potato wedges

4 large floury potatoes

2 tsp paprika

Good drizzle of vegetable oil

25g Parmesan cheese

Aïoli

3 garlic cloves

2 medium egg yolks

1 big pinch of English mustard powder

275ml sunflower oil

¼ lemon (optional)

Salad

2 tbsp extra virgin olive oil

1 tbsp white wine or balsamic vinegar

1 squidge of honey

½ tsp English mustard powder

100g baby spinach leaves

Cod burger

Drizzle of sunflower oil

1 tbsp plain flour

1 tbsp paprika

2 tsp ground cumin

1 tsp chilli powder

Few sprigs of fresh thyme (or you can use 2 tsp dried thyme or oregano here instead)

4 x 125g skinless, sustainably caught cod or pollack fillets

To serve

4 burger buns

Salt and freshly ground black pepper

Blackened Cajun cod burgers with aïoli & paprika baked potato wedges

I am quite partial to home-baked potato wedges, but if you are in a massive hurry, just use frozen chips sprinkled with a bit of paprika. I won't tell, if you don't!

+ Preheat the oven to 220°C, (fan 200°C), 425°F, Gas Mark 7 with the top shelf at the ready.

+ Cut each potato in half lengthways and then cut each piece into four or five long wedges. Toss them in a large baking tray with the paprika, oil and some salt and pepper. Arrange them in a single layer and roast in the oven for 30 minutes.

+ Meanwhile, make the aïoli. Peel the garlic cloves and blitz them in a food processor with the egg yolks and mustard powder. With the motor running, slowly add half the oil, drip by drip. Then gradually add the other half in a steady drizzle to make a thick, creamy mayonnaise. Add a squeeze of lemon juice to taste, if using, and set aside.

+ For the salad dressing, mix the olive oil, vinegar, honey and mustard powder together in a large bowl, season with salt and pepper to taste and set aside also.

+ Once the potatoes have been cooking for 15 minutes, pull them out of the oven, finely grate the Parmesan over the top and pop them back in for another 15 minutes.

+ Now, prepare the fish. Put a drizzle of oil in a large frying pan on a medium heat. Put the flour, paprika, ground cumin and chilli powder on a plate with some salt and pepper and toss together. Pick the leaves from the thyme and toss them in (or the dried thyme or oregano).

+ Coat the cod fillets well in the spiced flour, shaking off the excess. Add the fish to the pan and leave to cook for 4 minutes on the first side.

>

Blackened Cajun cod burgers with aïoli & paprika baked potato wedges

(continued)

+ After 4 minutes, flip the fish over to cook on the other side.

+ In the meantime, split the burger buns in half, place them cut side up on a baking tray and put them in the oven for a few minutes to crisp up a little.

+ Put the salad in a bowl, add the dressing and toss.

+ Check that the fish is cooked. The centre should be piping hot with shiny, opaque flesh through to the middle. Remove from the heat.

+ Remove the buns and potato wedges from the oven. The wedges should be tender on the inside and crisp and golden on the outside.

+ Sandwich the cod and aïoli between the buns. Serve with the potato wedges and a handful of the dressed leaves. Any spare aïoli will keep for 2 days in the fridge.

Time from start to finish:
30 minutes
Serves: 4
Equipment: Roasting tin, grater,
roasting tray, medium pan

Ginger butternut squash

2 x 320g bags of ready-prepared
butternut squash

2cm piece of fresh ginger

8 garlic cloves

A few fresh sage leaves

Couple of sprigs of fresh rosemary

Extra virgin olive oil

Fish

4 chunky, sustainably caught white fish
fillets (such as cod or pollack), skinless
if you don't fancy it

50g butter

Pancetta petits pois

100g cubed pancetta

300g frozen petits pois or peas

Small handful of fresh mint leaves
(optional), to serve

Salt and freshly ground black pepper

Buttered fish with roasted ginger butternut squash & pancetta petits pois

The supermarkets have started stocking ready-prepared butternut squash, which really gets my vote. Although there is something quite satisfying to me about seeing those little amber cubes of yumminess form from that big peanut-shaped veg, when time is of the essence, a little bit of help in a bag goes a long way.

+ Preheat the oven to 200°C, (fan 180°C), 400°F, Gas Mark 6.

+ Tip the squash into a roasting tin, peel the ginger and finely grate it over, scatter the unpeeled garlic cloves in, rip the sage leaves over and slide your fingers down the length of the rosemary to release the leaves and add them also.

+ Drizzle the whole thing with oil, then season well with salt and pepper and roast in the oven for 25 minutes.

+ Meanwhile, get on with the fish. Lay the fillets skin side down on a roasting tray. Cut the butter up into small pieces, reserve a knob, then arrange the rest on top of the fish fillets and season really well with salt and pepper.

+ When the squash has been cooking for 15 minutes, give it a little toss about and put the fish in the oven so that they will be ready at the same time.

+ As this cooks, prepare the petits pois. Put a little drizzle of oil in a medium pan on a medium to high heat. Once hot, add the pancetta and cook for about 3–4 minutes until crisp and golden. Then throw in the petits pois or peas, the reserved knob of butter and some salt and pepper to taste and let the whole thing cook away for about 5 minutes until the petits pois are tender.

>

Buttered fish with roasted ginger butternut squash & pancetta petits pois

(continued)

+ When everything is cooked, remove the squash and fish from the oven. To check that the fish is done, insert a knife into the thickest part and take a look inside. The flesh should be completely opaque through to the centre. The squash should be soft and caramelised on the edges.

+ Divide the squash between four serving plates. Put a piece of fish on top of each with the pancetta petits pois at the side. Drizzle over some oil if you fancy it, rip over the mint leaves, if using, and serve.

Fish + shellfish mains

Time from start to finish.
30 minutes
Serves: 4
Equipment: Medium sauté pan,
kettle, blender, medium bowl,
large frying pan, plate, colander

Bean mix

Drizzle of vegetable oil

1 large red onion

4 tsp balsamic vinegar

2 tsp caster sugar

400g tin of haricot beans, chickpeas
or flageolet beans

25g raisins

Pesto

Large handful of fresh coriander

Large handful of fresh flat leaf parsley

2 garlic cloves

50ml olive oil

2 tsp ground cumin

Cous cous

200g cous cous

Small handful of fresh mint

Handful (about 25g) of toasted pine
nuts (they are available from many
supermarkets ready toasted)

Large squidge of honey (optional)

Fish

Drizzle of vegetable oil

25g plain flour

1 tsp ground cumin

1 tsp ground coriander

1 tsp paprika

4 x 200g chunky, sustainably caught
fish fillets like cod or halibut, skin on

Salt and freshly ground black pepper

Moroccan pesto fish with caramelised onions & haricot beans served with minty pine nut cous cous

This Moroccan pesto is my take on charmoula, a classic North African marinade served with things such as chicken or fish. The flavours are really intense and this is a very filling, but healthy dish. The pesto can be made using a pestle and mortar if you don't have a blender — it does take some elbow grease, but it will still work. I freeze the leftover coriander and parsley stems and use them in soups and stocks for extra flavour.

+ Start with the bean mix. Put a medium sauté pan with a good drizzle of oil on a medium heat. Peel and finely slice the onion and then add to the hot oil with the balsamic vinegar, caster sugar and some salt and pepper and cook for about 10 minutes, stirring from time to time.

+ Put the kettle on for the cous cous and start the pesto while waiting.

+ Rip the leaves from the bunches of coriander and parsley and peel the garlic cloves. Place both in a blender with the oil and cumin, then blitz to a paste and set aside.

+ Tip the cous cous into a medium bowl and pour the now-boiled water over to just cover. Cover with cling film and leave to sit for 8 minutes while you cook the fish.

+ Drizzle some oil into a large frying pan over a high heat. Put the flour on a plate and toss through the cumin, coriander, paprika and some salt and pepper. Coat the fillets of fish all over with it, shaking off the excess. Place them, skin side up, into the hot oil and leave to cook for 3 minutes.

+ Now the onions should be lovely and soft. Drain and rinse the beans and stir them into the onions with the raisins and a good amount of salt and pepper. Leave to cook for a few minutes more.

>

Moroccan pesto fish with caramelised onions & haricot beans served with minty pine nut cous cous

(continued)

+ After the fish fillets have cooked for 3 minutes, carefully flip them over and leave to cook for another 5 minutes.

+ Check the cous cous — it should be nice and tender, so fluff it up with a fork. Rip the mint leaves off the stalks and add them to the cous cous with the pine nuts and honey, if using. Season with salt and pepper to taste.

+ Check to see if the fish is cooked by cutting a little slit into the middle — it should be opaque right through to the centre.

+ Divide the cous cous between four serving plates. Place a piece of fish on top, followed by a spoonful of the bean mix and finally some Moroccan pesto.

Time from start to finish:
35 minutes
Serves: 4
Equipment: 2 large sauté pans,
large frying pan, colander

Potatoes

Olive oil

1kg potatoes

4 sprigs of fresh rosemary

4 garlic cloves

Sauce

1 aubergine

2 celery sticks

1 bunch of spring onions

150g sundried tomatoes

400g tin of cherry tomatoes

1 tbsp caster sugar

50ml balsamic vinegar

Pinch of chilli flakes (optional)

Handful (about 75g) of pitted green olives (optional; I know lots of people don't like them)

Handful (about 2 tbsp) of toasted pine nuts (you can buy them ready toasted from the supermarket)

Fish

4–6 x 100g (approx) sustainably caught sea bass fillets (or any other white fish will work too), skin on

Small handful of fresh basil, to serve

Salt and freshly ground black pepper

Pan-fried sea bass with basil & pine nut sweet veggie sauce & rosemary sautéed potatoes

This sweet Spanish sauce is called samfaina and is similar to the French ratatouille or the Italian caponata. Each is a type of vegetable stew with varying ingredients depending on the region. The beauty of this sauce is that you can make extra and use it on pasta or bruschettas, or serve it with most meats from pork to lamb. Once you have made it a couple of times, it can be fun to have a play with it, adding your own variants as you fancy.

+ Pour the oil to about 5mm deep in a large sauté pan set over a medium heat.

+ Meanwhile, peel the potatoes and cut them into about 2cm cubes, strip the leaves from the rosemary stalks and bash three of the garlic cloves with the side of a knife to squash them (but leave the skin on).

+ Once the oil is hot, carefully add the potatoes, half of the rosemary and three of the garlic cloves. Lower the heat and leave to cook gently for about 25 minutes, stirring them from time to time so they cook evenly and don't burn.

+ Pour a drizzle of oil into a large sauté pan and place it on a low to medium heat. Trim and cut the aubergine into bite sized pieces and add to the pan. Adding them to the pan as you go along, trim and finely chop the celery sticks, spring onions (both the green and the white bits) and peel and finely chop the remaining clove of garlic. Give everything a good stir and sauté for 1–2 minutes.

+ Roughly chop the sundried tomatoes and add to the pan with the tinned cherry tomatoes, caster sugar, balsamic vinegar, chilli flakes and green olives, if using, pine nuts and the reserved rosemary.

>

Pan-fried sea bass with basil & pine nut sweet veggie sauce & rosemary sautéed potatoes

(continued)

+ Stir everything together and bring to a simmer, then leave to cook for about 10 minutes, stirring from time to time so that it doesn't catch on the bottom.

+ Drizzle a little oil into a large frying pan on a medium heat. Slash the sea bass skin a few times with a sharp knife and season both sides with salt and pepper. Put the fish skin side down in the pan and leave to cook for 3 minutes.

+ The sauce should now be reduced and the vegetables softened. Taste the sauce, adjust the seasoning if necessary and turn the heat off.

+ Line a colander with kitchen paper and tip the cooked potatoes in. Season them with salt and pepper and leave them to drain for a moment.

+ Turn the fish over (the skin should be lovely and crispy) and leave to fry for a further 2 minutes until cooked through.

+ Divide the potatoes between four serving plates, top each with a fillet of sea bass and then spoon the sauce over. Rip the basil leaves over to serve.

Time from start to finish:
25 minutes
Serves: 4
Equipment: Large sauté pan,
pestle and mortar (or a mug and
rolling pin), kettle, large pan with
lid, colander

2 tsp fennel seeds

150g spicy chorizo ring

2 sprigs of fresh rosemary

2 garlic cloves

1 red chilli

Olive oil

2 x 400g tins of chopped tomatoes

1 glass of Cabernet Sauvignon (or
other red wine or a good fish or
chicken stock)

1 tbsp harissa paste (or tomato purée
if you don't like it too hot)

2 tsp dried oregano

300g linguine pasta

225g sustainably caught peeled
prawns (preferably raw but cooked
will work too)

2 tsp caster sugar (optional)

Small handful of fresh flat leaf parsley,
to serve

Salt and freshly ground black pepper

Prawn linguine with chorizo & Cabernet tomato sauce

I am a chorizo lover. I cannot get enough of it. I think
not a day goes by without me eating some of it. Really!
If you can't get your hands on a chorizo 'ring' then any
flavourful sausage will do. Try some venison sausage or
those made with pork and caramelised red onion, which
are a great substitute.

+ Put a large sauté pan on a medium heat (with no oil in for the moment).
Bash up the fennel seeds using a pestle and mortar (or in a mug with the
end of a rolling pin) until lightly crushed and tip them into the pan. Cook
for 3–4 minutes, tossing them from time to time until they start to release
their lovely smell.

+ Meanwhile, slit the chorizo down the side, peel and discard the casing
and cut the sausage into chunks. Pull your fingers down the length of the
rosemary to release the leaves and then finely chop them. Peel and finely
chop the garlic and deseed and finely chop the chilli. Add everything to
the now sweet-smelling fennel with a little drizzle of oil and cook for
1–2 minutes, stirring

+ Next add the tomatoes, wine (or stock), harissa paste (or tomato purée)
and oregano. Then whack up the heat and leave it to bubble away for
about 15 minutes so the sauce can become nice and thick and full of
flavour. Give it a stir every so often to prevent it sticking.

+ As this cooks, put the kettle on to boil and then cook the linguine in a
large pan according to the packet instructions.

+ Add the prawns to the sauce for the last 4–5 minutes of cooking time. If
using already cooked prawns, they will take a little less time as you are
simply warming them through.

+ Meanwhile, drain the cooked pasta well and return it to the pan, adding
a good drizzle of oil and some salt and pepper, then pop the lid on to
keep warm.

>

Prawn linguine with chorizo & Cabernet tomato sauce

(continued)

+ The prawns should now be cooked in the sauce. They should be pink and white on the outside and white inside. Taste the sauce, adding some salt and pepper if you think it needs it and a little sugar if it tastes too sharp. If you add sugar, stir it in well and then leave to cook for another minute.

+ Finally, tip the sauce into the pasta, stir well, then divide between four plates, scatter with the ripped-up parsley and serve.

Tin foil Thai trout with red pepper noodles

Time from start to finish:
30 minutes
Serves: 4
Equipment: Peeler, baking tray, medium wok or sauté pan

Fish

1 bunch of spring onions

2cm piece of fresh ginger

1 red chilli

1 celery stick

1 carrot

1 garlic clove

½ bag of fresh coriander

4 sustainably caught trout fillets (about 125g each)

4 tsp soy sauce

4 tsp sesame oil

2 limes

Noodles

Sesame oil

1 red pepper

2 x 150g packs of straight-to-wok medium noodles

2 tbsp soy sauce (optional)

Salt and freshly ground black pepper

Not strictly Thai, but with a nod to its flavours nonetheless. A fun and healthy way to cook a delicious piece of trout, but it can also be replaced with salmon. I've used tin foil here, but baking parchment makes a good alternative.

+ Preheat the oven to 200°C, (fan 180°C), 400°F, Gas Mark 6.

+ Trim the spring onions and then cut them in half, dividing the green and the white bits. Cut each spring onion in half lengthways and set aside. Peel and finely slice the ginger and cut into thin strips. Deseed the chilli and cut into long, thin strips also. Halve the celery stick and peel the carrot and cut both into thin, finger-length sticks. Peel and finely slice the garlic and cut the stalks off the coriander (keeping the leaves and stalks separate).

+ Tear off four 34cm squares (approximately) of tin foil and lay them out individually. Put a piece of trout in the centre of each one. Divide all the prepared vegetables between each one, scattering them over. Only use the coriander stalks for now, reserving the leaves for serving. Drizzle the soy sauce and sesame oil over, squeeze in the juice of one of the limes and season with a little salt and pepper.

+ Now wrap the trout up in the tin foil. Any way will do just as long as the foil is well sealed, but not too taut, so air can circulate and steam the fish. Place the parcels on a baking tray and put in the oven for 12 minutes.

+ A few minutes before the fish is ready, cook the noodles. Put some sesame oil in a medium wok or sauté pan and get it nice and hot. Halve, deseed and finely slice the red pepper and then stir-fry for 1 minute. Add the noodles and continue to stir-fry for 2 minutes until they are piping hot. Add some soy sauce to taste if you fancy it and then season well with salt, pepper and a drizzle of sesame oil.

+ Divide the noodles between four serving plates. Remove the trout from the oven and serve in the foil parcels next to the noodles. Quarter the remaining lime and nestle a piece into each one. Serve scattered with the reserved coriander leaves.

Time from start to finish:
20 minutes
Serves: 2
Equipment: Kettle, small pan,
medium pan with tight-fitting lid,
small bowl

2 medium eggs

300g basmati or long grain rice

2 tsp curry powder

½ tsp ground turmeric

1 bunch of spring onions

Small handful of fresh chives

125g pack of hot-smoked trout
(it is ready to eat)

50g butter

A few fresh basil leaves, to serve

Dressing

2 tbsp half- or full-fat crème fraîche

½ lemon

Salt and freshly ground black pepper

Hot–smoked trout kedgeree with spring onions & basil

I am not ashamed to admit that I only discovered hot-smoked trout a few months ago at the supermarket. A great find for a quick and tasty meal. Rub the fish up and down with your fingers before you use it to check for the odd bone that may be there. A truly sumptuous supper dish or one for a decadent breakfast.

+ Put the kettle on to boil for the rice.

+ Place the eggs in a small pan and cover with water. Put on a high heat and as soon as the water comes to the boil, let it bubble away for 4 minutes for almost-hard-boiled eggs.

+ Tip the rice, curry powder and turmeric into a medium pan. Pour over enough boiled water to come about 2cm above the rice (roughly 500ml of water, to be pedantic). Cover with the lid and return to the boil. Then reduce the heat to low and leave to cook for as long as it says on the packet.

+ Meanwhile, slice up the spring onions (both the green and the white bits), finely chop the chives and break the fish into bite-sized flakes (removing any fine bones that you find) and set aside.

+ Once the eggs are ready, drain them and run them under a cold tap for a moment to stop them from cooking. Peel, cut them into quarters and set them aside.

+ Next prepare the dressing. Simply spoon the crème fraîche into a small bowl and squeeze the lemon juice in. Season with salt and pepper to taste and stir everything together (it should be quite thin, for drizzling).

+ Check the rice is tender and fluff it up with a fork. Add the butter and let it melt for a moment before stirring it through. Add the spring onions, chives and smoked trout. Season to taste with salt and pepper and gently stir everything together.

+ Divide the rice between two serving bowls, arrange the egg quarters on top and drizzle the dressing over. Scatter the basil over and serve.

Time from start to finish:
10–15 minutes
Serves: 4
Equipment: Large bowl, colander,
large frying pan, mug or small
bowl

300g cherry tomatoes

1 small red onion

2 x 400g tins of cannellini beans

Large handful of capers

200g feta cheese

Sunflower oil

4 large sustainably caught tuna steaks
(about 2cm thick)

Dressing

4 tbsp extra virgin olive oil

2 tbsp balsamic vinegar

Drizzle of maple syrup or honey

1 lime

Small handful of fresh mint, to serve

Salt and freshly ground black pepper

Seared tuna steaks with cannellini beans, feta & mint

This is quite a summery dish, but also perfect for those days when perhaps you fancy something a little lighter. You could also try it with rice instead of cannellini beans if you feel like a change.

+ Cut the tomatoes in half and put them into a large bowl. Peel and finely slice up the red onion, drain and rinse the beans, rinse the capers and add these too. Finally, crumble the feta in.

+ Drizzle some oil into a large frying pan and get it nice and hot over a high heat.

+ While this heats up, season the tuna well with salt and pepper, really getting a good amount on. Then lower them into the hot oil. Cook for 1 minute per side for rare, 2 minutes for medium and 3 minutes for well done.

+ Meanwhile, make the salad dressing. Put the oil, balsamic vinegar, maple syrup or honey and salt and pepper into a mug or small bowl and whisk with a fork. Pour over the salad, toss well and divide between four plates.

+ Check the tuna is cooked to your liking and remove from the heat. Lay a tuna steak on top of each salad portion, quarter the lime and place a piece to the side of each. Then rip over the mint leaves and serve.

Time from start to finish:
15 minutes
Serves: 2
Equipment: Medium frying pan,
large frying pan, sieve, mug

Vegetable oil

2 x 125g (approx) sustainably caught
salmon fillets, skin on

75g spicy chorizo ring

100g asparagus tips (or green beans)

400g tin of puy or green lentils

2 sprigs of fresh rosemary

Dressing

5 tbsp extra virgin olive oil

3 tbsp balsamic vinegar

1 tbsp maple syrup

Pinch of English mustard powder
or small dollop of Dijon mustard
(optional)

Salt and freshly ground black pepper

Warm salmon & lentils with chorizo, asparagus & a balsamic dressing

I did a big Twitter survey earlier in the year to ask my followers how many frying pans they had. Surprisingly, the answer came back as three on average, which is more than the two I have at home! If you don't have two frying pans, then cook the lentil salad in a medium-sized saucepan. It will just mean a bit more stirring to make sure that everything is cooked, but it will still taste the same. Cook the fish in another pan skin side down, so the skin crisps up and protects the fish from drying out. I love this at any time of year, when a warm, salady dish is just the thing for my mood.

+ Put a medium frying pan, with a good drizzle of oil in, plus a large frying pan, without oil in, on a medium heat.

+ As they heat up, dab the salmon fillets dry with some kitchen paper (this helps the fish skin crisp up nicely) and then season with salt and pepper. Then lower the fish, skin side down, into the pan with hot oil and leave to cook, untouched, for 5 minutes.

+ Meanwhile, make a slit down the side of the chorizo and use your hands to peel the skin off. Then cut it into bite-sized chunks and set aside.

+ Lay the asparagus in one bunch on the chopping board and cut off the hard woody ends all in one go. If using green beans, trim the stalk end of each. Toss the asparagus (or green beans) into the hot dry frying pan and leave them to cook for about 2 minutes, tossing all the time so they cook evenly. Then add the chorizo, reduce the heat to low and cook for about 3 minutes, tossing every so often.

+ By now, the fish has probably been frying for about 5 minutes (and the skin is hopefully nice and crispy), so flip it over and leave to cook for another 5 minutes on the other side.

>

Warm salmon & lentils with chorizo, asparagus & a balsamic dressing

(continued)

+ Drain the lentils in a sieve and give them a good rinse. Run your fingers down the length of the rosemary stalks to release the leaves and then finely chop them. Add both ingredients to the chorizo pan and leave to cook for about 5 minutes, stirring every now and again.

+ To make the dressing, place the oil, vinegar, maple syrup and mustard in a mug, add salt and pepper, then whisk together with a fork and set aside.

+ Now check that the fish is cooked. It should be just opaque and nice and hot in the centre. Remove from the heat.

+ Check that the lentils and chorizo are piping hot, season them to taste and then divide them between two plates. Sit a piece of salmon, skin side up, on top of each. Drizzle the dressing over and serve.

Salmon saltimbocca with gremolata potatoes & crispy sage leaves

Time from start to finish:
30 minutes
Serves: 4
Equipment: Kettle, jug or stick blender, zester, large pan with lid, large frying pan, colander, masher or rolling pin

Gremolata potatoes

Large handful of fresh flat leaf parsley
2 garlic cloves
1 lemon
1 tbsp olive oil
750g baby new potatoes
Knob of butter
Handful of toasted pine nuts (they come ready toasted from the supermarket)

Fish

8 slices of prosciutto or pancetta
4 x 125g (approx) preferably skinless, sustainably caught salmon fillets
16 good-sized fresh sage leaves
Vegetable oil

Salad

1 bag of baby spinach leaves
A drizzle of extra virgin olive oil
A drizzle of balsamic vinegar
1 large handful of sundried tomatoes
Salt and freshly ground black pepper

My dad, who speaks many, many languages, tells me that in Italian saltimbocca literally means 'to jump in the mouth'. So this is 'jump in your mouth salmon'. It is a traditional European dish usually made with meat wrapped up in sage and prosciutto. Lots of people say that they are not really good at cooking fish. For me fish cooking is all about practice and experimenting. After a few goes at cooking it, the fish will be just right and then it will begin to come naturally.

+ Put the kettle on to boil for the potatoes. While you are waiting, get started on preparing the gremolata. Rip the parsley leaves off the stalks and place in a blender (a stick blender works a treat and is less hassle to wash up!). Peel and add the garlic, grate the lemon zest in and add the oil.

+ Tip the potatoes into a large pan and pour the boiling water over to cover. Put the lid on, bring back to the boil and then when the pan lid starts to rattle, turn the heat down and leave them to simmer for 15–20 minutes until tender.

+ Now back to the gremolata. Briefly whiz the ingredients in the blender until combined. Season to taste with salt and pepper and set aside.

+ Next prepare the salmon. Lay two slices of prosciutto or pancetta overlapping lengthways. Sit a piece of salmon, round side up, near one short edge. Season with salt and pepper and arrange three sage leaves along the length of the fish. Roll the prosciutto around the salmon until completely wrapped. Repeat until all four are wrapped (you should have four sage leaves left over, which will get used shortly).

+ Put a large frying pan on a high heat and add a little oil. Once hot, place the fillets in, sage leaf side down, turn the heat to medium and leave them to cook for about 3 minutes.

>

Salmon saltimbocca with gremolata potatoes & crispy sage leaves

(continued)

+ While the fish cooks, throw in the remaining sage leaves. They crisp up in seconds. Then, remove them with tongs or a slotted spoon onto kitchen paper to drain the excess oil off.

+ Now flip the salmon over and leave to cook for another 6 minutes on the other side.

+ Check on the potatoes — a knife should glide through to the centre. Once they are cooked, drain them well and return to the pan. Add some salt and pepper, a big knob of butter, the gremolata, crisp fried sage leaves and the pine nuts. Now I like to use a masher or end of a rolling pin to very gently crush (rather than mash) the potatoes so they are still fairly whole. Put the lid on to keep them warm.

+ To check the salmon is cooked, cut a little slit underneath through to the centre. The flesh should be just turning opaque and pale pink all the way through. If so, remove the pan from the heat.

+ Divide the potatoes between four plates and top with a piece of salmon. For the salad, place a handful of spinach leaves to the side, drizzle with oil and balsamic vinegar, scatter the sundried tomatoes over and serve.

Filo salmon en croute with basil & curly kale pesto & pesto potatoes

Time from start to finish: 35 minutes
Serves: 4
Equipment: Kettle, grater, stick or jug blender or food processor, large pan with lid, small bowl or mug, pastry brush, 2 baking trays, colander, masher

1kg baby new potatoes
4 x 125g (approx) skinless, sustainably caught salmon fillets
2 sheets of filo pastry
Extra virgin olive oil
4 vines of cherry tomatoes

Pesto

50g Parmesan cheese
Large handful of fresh basil
2 garlic cloves
75g toasted pine nuts (you can buy them ready toasted)
Large handful of curly kale (about 50g)
150ml extra virgin olive oil
Salt and freshly ground black pepper

I have just bought a stick (or immersion) blender, which has become my favourite new toy. Put all the ingredients into a tall jug, stick the blender in and blitz. A fabulous invention and the perfect piece of kitchen equipment for a very quick, creamy pesto.

+ Preheat the oven to 220°C, (fan 200°C), 425°F, Gas Mark 7, and put a kettle on for the potatoes.

+ Start by making the pesto. Finely grate the Parmesan, pick the leaves from the basil stalks, peel and roughly chop the garlic and put it all into a bowl, blender or food processor. Add the toasted pine nuts, kale and finally the oil, then blitz until smooth, season with salt and pepper to taste and set aside.

+ Tip the potatoes into a large pan, pour the now-boiled water from the kettle over to cover and add a little salt. Put the lid on, bring back to the boil and leave to bubble away for 15–20 minutes.

+ Season each salmon fillet well with salt and pepper and then spread a teaspoon of pesto on top of each one.

+ Cut the filo pastry sheets in half across. Place a salmon fillet, pesto side down, in the middle of one of the pieces of pastry. Pour a little oil into a small bowl or mug and brush it all around the edge of the pastry. Wrap the pastry around the salmon to enclose, just as you would wrap a present. Repeat to make three more parcels, arranging them pesto side up on a baking tray as they are finished.

+ Arrange the vines of cherry tomatoes on another baking tray, season them with salt and pepper and drizzle a little oil over. Bake both in the oven for 12–14 minutes.

+ Meanwhile, check on the potatoes. To test they are cooked, slide a knife into one of the bigger potatoes. It should glide through without any give.

>

Filo salmon en croute with basil & curly kale pesto & pesto potatoes

(continued)

+ When cooked, drain the potatoes and return them to the pan. Add the remaining pesto and then crush the potatoes gently with a masher. Season with salt and pepper to taste and then divide between four plates.

+ The salmon should now be cooked through with crisp, golden pastry and the tomatoes softened and just beginning to catch colour. Remove them from the oven and place a salmon parcel on top of each pile of potatoes with a vine of cooked tomatoes beside and serve.

Honey soy-glazed salmon with sesame & ginger noodles & stir-fried bok choy

Time from start to finish:
25 minutes
Serves: **4**
Equipment: **Peeler, large frying pan, wok or sauté pan, mug or small bowl**

200g bok choy

1 bunch of spring onions

2cm piece of fresh ginger

Sesame oil

4 x 125g sustainably caught salmon fillets, skin on

3 squidges of honey

100ml light soy sauce

Pinch of chilli flakes or powder

1 lime

300g straight-to-wok noodles

1 tbsp sesame seeds

Small handful of fresh coriander leaves, to serve

Salt and freshly ground black pepper

I realise this recipe is not going to reinvent the wheel, but it is a staple in my house, which comes in handy when my daughter comes home from school, nearly always ravenous from a high-octane day and in need of something quick and tasty with plenty of carbs. Trout fillets, which I have just started using a lot of, make a good alternative to salmon.

+ Trim the bok choy to release the leaves, then rinse and pat them dry with kitchen paper. Trim and roughly chop the spring onions (both the green and the white bits) and peel and grate the ginger.

+ Put a large frying pan and a wok or sauté pan on a medium heat with a small glug of sesame oil in each.

+ Season the salmon fillets well with salt and pepper, and fry them skin side up in the frying pan for 5 minutes.

+ Meanwhile, stir-fry the bok choy, spring onions and ginger in the wok or sauté pan for about 3 minutes until the leaves are wilted.

+ While these are frying, quickly put the honey, soy sauce and chilli flakes or powder into a mug or small bowl and whisk everything together with a fork. Quarter the lime and set both aside.

+ Next carefully flip the fish fillets over to cook on the other side for about 4 minutes.

+ Add the noodles and sesame seeds to the vegetables and toss together well, then continue to cook for a few more minutes, keeping everything moving around regularly.

>

Honey soy-glazed salmon with sesame & ginger noodles & stir-fried bok choy

(continued)

+ Turn the heat up on the salmon and pour half of the honey sauce over. Allow to simmer for a couple of minutes, spooning the sauce over the salmon as the mixture thickens and becomes syrupy.

+ Pour the remaining sauce over the noodles, tossing it through well, and then season with salt and pepper to taste.

+ The salmon is cooked when it is no longer translucent but an even pale pink through to the centre.

+ Divide the noodles between four serving plates. Sit a salmon fillet on top, drizzle some of the syrupy sauce from the pan over and serve with a wedge of lime and a scattering of coriander leaves.

Vegetarian mains

'Be brave. Take risks. Nothing can substitute experience.'
Paulo Coelho

In my teens I went veggie. It was a real 'right on' thing to do. A gaggle of girlie crusaders on a meat-free mission, we were the talk of the school and the talk of the tiny town in which I grew up. I do so wish, however, without the risk of blowing my own trumpet, that I had had a few simple recipes like these to cook once a week to get away from the omnipresent jacket potato with cheese or pasta with tomato sauce that I used to eat day in, day out! These are a few family favourites, which have proven very successful both for casual everyday meals and also those rare occasions when mates come over for a tasty bite.

Time from start to finish:
15 minutes
Serves: 4 as a snack (or makes
16 triangles for canapés)
Equipment: 2 medium frying
pans, pestle and mortar (or a
mug and rolling pin), baking
sheet, medium bowl

Sunflower oil

4 tbsp roasted chopped hazelnuts
(these come ready roasted and
chopped at most supermarkets)

Small handful of fresh coriander

4 corn or wheat tortillas

250g goat's cheese

4 tsp runny honey

1 bag of wild rocket

Extra virgin olive oil

A drizzle of balsamic vinegar

Salt and freshly ground black pepper

Goat's cheese, toasted hazelnut & honey quesadillas with rocket salad

The other day, my dad rang me to tell me that he had never been a fan of goat's cheese and always preferred the blue cheese of Stilton and Dolcelatte. But whilst he was at one of his many evenings of culture, he had been offered some goat's cheese drizzled with honey and had instantly fallen deeply in love with the perfect balance of flavours. So, dad, this one is for you.

+ Preheat the oven to 110°C, (fan 90°C), 225°F, Gas Mark ¼.

+ Put two medium frying pans (each wide enough to fit one of your tortillas in flat) on a medium heat with a tiny drizzle of sunflower oil in each.

+ While waiting for them to heat up, bash up the hazelnuts with a pestle and mortar (or in a mug with the end of a rolling pin). Pick and roughly chop the coriander leaves.

+ Place a tortilla into each of the pans and leave to toast for 1 minute. Then crumble over a quarter of the goat's cheese and scatter a quarter of the hazelnuts and coriander over one half of each one. Drizzle a little honey over, season with a little salt and pepper and fold the tortilla over to enclose the filling. Squish them down a bit with a spatula or fish slice, reduce the heat to low and leave to cook for a minute before flipping over and cooking for 5 minutes on the other side.

+ Slide them out of the pans onto a baking sheet and place in the oven to keep warm while you prepare the other two in the same way.

+ While the last two are cooking, tip the rocket leaves into a medium bowl. Drizzle over a bit of olive oil and balsamic vinegar. Scatter in some salt and pepper and then toss everything together.

+ Remove the tortillas from the oven. I like to cut each one into four and serve with the dressed rocket as a canapé or starter for a Mexican feast.

Prep time: 25 minutes
Time baking in the oven:
15–20 minutes
Serves: 4
Equipment: Kettle, grater, 2 small
bowls, large pan with lid, large
pan, medium bowl, masher,
25.5cm-square baking dish at
least 6cm deep (about 2.5 litres),
baking tray

50g Parmesan cheese

50g dried natural breadcrumbs

600g prepared sweet potato and
butternut squash

4 sprigs of fresh rosemary

12 sage leaves

Olive oil

12 lasagne sheets

100g toasted pine nuts (the
supermarket sells them ready toasted)

75g baby spinach leaves

White sauce

100g Parmesan cheese

2cm piece of fresh ginger

600g ricotta cheese

2 medium egg yolks

Pinch of freshly grated nutmeg

Salad

3 tbsp extra virgin olive oil

1 tbsp balsamic vinegar

Pinch of English mustard powder
(optional)

1 bag of wild rocket

Salt and freshly ground black pepper

Butternut & sweet potato lasagne with sage, toasted pine nuts & nutmeg

This is one of my stalwart recipes that used to only make an appearance when there was a vegetarian over at my house. But then the family began to fall in love with the soft wintry flavours and that creamy white sauce. This white sauce is a shortcut white sauce, everything just gets put in a bowl and stirred — very, very simple and just as tasty as the traditional version.

+ Preheat the oven to 220°C, (fan 200°C), 425°F, Gas Mark 7. Put the kettle on to boil for the vegetables.

+ While waiting for that, finely grate the Parmesan for the topping, toss in a small bowl along with the breadcrumbs and set aside.

+ When the kettle has boiled, tip the prepared sweet potato and butternut squash into a large pan, add a little salt and then pour the boiled water over to cover. Put the lid on, bring back to the boil and then leave to bubble away for 15–20 minutes until tender.

+ Fill the kettle up with water again and pop it back on to boil.

+ While waiting for the kettle, quickly prepare the herbs for later. Run your fingers down the length of the rosemary stalks to release the leaves, roughly chop them with the sage leaves and set aside in a small bowl

+ Pour the now-boiled water into a large pan, add a drizzle of oil, slip in the lasagne sheets and leave to cook for 5 minutes. (As there isn't loads of liquid in this dish, the lasagne sheets do need a bit of precooking even if they are 'no precook' lasagne sheets!)

+ In the meantime, prepare the sauce. Finely grate the Parmesan and peel and grate the ginger. Place both in a medium bowl, add the ricotta, egg yolks and nutmeg, season with salt and pepper, then stir to combine and set aside.

>

Butternut & sweet potato lasagne with sage, toasted pine nuts & nutmeg

(continued)

+ Once the lasagne sheets have cooked for 5 minutes, drain them and tip them back into the pan. Drizzle in a little more oil and gently toss them about to coat, so that the sheets don't stick together.

+ Check that the vegetables are now nice and tender. Drain them off well and tip them back into the pan. Mash them with a masher until smooth and add salt and pepper to taste.

+ Now assemble the lasagne in the baking dish, set on a baking tray. Spread a third of the vegetable mash in the base of the dish. Next, scatter a third of the herbs, pine nuts and spinach leaves over. Then arrange four lasagne sheets on top, cutting to fit if necessary. Spread a third of the ricotta mix over.

+ Repeat this twice more, giving you three layers, and finally sprinkle the Parmesan breadcrumbs on top. Bake for 15–20 minutes.

+ While that is cooking, prepare the salad dressing by simply mixing the olive oil, balsamic vinegar, mustard powder (if using) and seasoning together in a small bowl.

+ When the lasagne is ready, the pasta will feel tender when pierced through with a knife and the top will be crisp and golden.

+ Cut it into portions, carefully lift out and serve with a handful of rocket drizzled with the dressing.

Prep time: **25 minutes**
Time baking in the oven:
20–25 minutes
Serves: **4–6**
Equipment: **Really large pan with lid, small pan (or small bowl and microwave), 23cm springform tin, baking sheet, sieve, pastry brush, baking tray**

Vegetable oil

1 bunch of spring onions

1 garlic clove

600g baby spinach leaves

50g butter

200g feta cheese

Small handful of fresh dill

200g cream cheese

50g toasted pine nuts (you can buy them ready toasted from the supermarket)

50g raisins

3 medium eggs

Big pinch of freshly grated nutmeg

6 sheets of filo pastry

4–6 small vines of cherry tomatoes

Extra virgin olive oil

Salt and freshly ground black pepper

Greek spinach, feta & pine nut pie with dill & crunchy filo

An impressive-looking pie. Great hot from the oven or for a packed lunch in the office. Mini ones can be fun to make also: just use a cupcake tray and line each hole with filo, add the filling and then top with another piece of this superfine pastry.

+ Preheat the oven to 200°C, (fan 180°C), 400°F, Gas Mark 6.

+ Place a really large pan with a drizzle of vegetable oil on a medium heat. Trim and finely slice the spring onions (the green and white bits), peel and finely chop the garlic and add them to the pan along with the spinach and some salt and pepper. Put the lid on and leave to cook for a few minutes until completely wilted, tossing from time to time.

+ Meanwhile, melt the butter in a small pan or in a small bowl in the microwave. Use some of it to grease the inside of the springform tin and set aside on a baking sheet.

+ Tip the wilted spinach into a sieve and leave it for a few minutes until cool enough to handle.

+ Whilst that cools, crumble the feta cheese into bite-sized pieces. Trim the dill stalks off and discard and then roughly chop the leaves.

+ Going back to the spinach mixture, get your hands in and squeeze as much liquid as possible out of it.

+ Return the spinach mixture to the pan (turn the heat off), add the feta, dill, cream cheese, pine nuts and raisins. Crack the eggs in, add the nutmeg and some salt and pepper (not too much salt as the feta is pretty salty). Mix everything together gently. At this stage in the proceedings the mixture won't look like the most beautiful thing in the world, but after a little magic in the oven it will come good.

>

Spicy bean burgers with corn cous cous & coriander lime crème fraîche

(continued)

+ Once the underside of the burgers are lovely and crisp and golden, flip them over carefully (as they are softer than regular meat burgers). Drizzle some oil into the pan if dry and leave the burgers to cook on the other side for 5 minutes.

+ Meanwhile, cut the cherry tomatoes in half and drain the sweetcorn well. Check the cous cous is tender and, if so, fluff up with a fork. Add the tomatoes, sweetcorn and drizzle with the rest of the extra virgin olive oil. Season to taste with salt and pepper and cover again to keep warm.

+ Peel and slice the red onion into rings and set aside for a moment. Cut the avocado in half, remove the stone (see page 45), peel off the skin and cut the avocado into slices.

+ Spoon the cous cous out onto each serving plate. Check the burgers are crisp and golden on the other side and remove them from the pan onto the cous cous. Arrange the avocado slices and onion rings on the tops of the burgers. Dollop the crème fraîche sauce on top, scatter the remaining coriander leaves over and serve.

Time from start to finish:
30 minutes
Serves: 4–6
Equipment: 23cm non-stick
frying pan with lid, peeler,
medium jug, heatproof rubber
spatula

Sunflower oil

1 medium sweet potato

1 courgette

1 bunch of spring onions

100g chestnut mushrooms

1–2 garlic cloves

1 red pepper

75g sliced red jalapeños (you can find
them ready sliced in jars from most
supermarkets)

12 medium eggs

100g tinned or frozen and defrosted
sweetcorn

Salt and freshly ground black pepper

To serve

1 bag of mixed salad leaves

Extra virgin olive oil

Balsamic vinegar

Small handful of fresh dill

Small handful of fresh basil

Sweet potato tortilla with jalapeños & dill

You will need a lid for your pan in this spicy Spanish-inspired recipe, but if you don't have one, then cover tightly with tin foil or use a heavy baking tray on top instead. Also, ensure the pan has a heatproof handle as it will be going under the grill.

+ Preheat the oven to 180°C, (fan 160°C), 350°F, Gas Mark 4. Put some oil in the frying pan on a low to medium heat. Peel the sweet potato and cut into rounds, just under 5mm thick. Toss into the frying pan, put the lid on and cook gently for about 8 minutes, stirring occasionally.

+ While this cooks, trim and finely slice the courgette, spring onions (the green and white bits) and mushrooms and peel and finely slice the garlic. Halve and deseed the pepper and slice into strips. Drain the jalapeños well on kitchen paper and set everything aside for a moment.

+ Check the sweet potato and, when just soft, add the prepared vegetables and sauté for 4–5 minutes until beginning to soften.

+ Meanwhile, crack the eggs into a medium jug, beat together and season with a good amount of salt and pepper (it really needs lots of seasoning). Then, once the vegetables are ready, pour the eggs evenly over and scatter the sweetcorn (drained if tinned) on top. Turn the heat down to really low, pop the lid on (see my note above) and cook for about 8 minutes.

+ When the tortilla is almost cooked, set the grill to a medium heat. Once the eggs are cooked at the edge but still a little wet in the middle, remove them from the heat and remove the lid. Slide under the grill to cook the top for 3–4 minutes. Move the pan to a lower shelf if it is cooking too quickly (you want the egg to cook through to the centre, not just the top).

+ Meanwhile, tip the salad leaves into a large salad-serving bowl. Drizzle a little olive oil and balsamic vinegar over and set aside for a moment.

+ Once the eggs are just set with a slight wobble in the middle, remove the tortilla from the grill. Using a heatproof rubber spatula, carefully slide the tortilla out of the pan and onto a serving board or plate. Tear some dill and basil leaves over and serve straight to the table with the salad.

Time from start to finish:
45 minutes
Serves: 4
Equipment: Grater, blender or
food processor, medium bowl,
large frying pan, large bowl

Pesto

25g Parmesan cheese

1 garlic clove (preferably roasted)

2 x 30g packs of fresh basil

50ml extra virgin olive oil

50g toasted pine nuts (they come
ready toasted from the supermarket)

Gnocchi

100g Parmesan cheese

Small handful of fresh thyme sprigs
(or 1 tbsp of dried oregano)

350g mascarpone

300g plain flour, plus extra for dusting

2 medium eggs

Olive oil

50g butter

To serve

1 bag of wild rocket

25g toasted pine nuts

1 lemon

Salt and freshly ground black pepper

Pan-fried mascarpone gnocchi with dreamy basil pesto

I first had gnocchi in an Italian restaurant near my house and I had to find out all about it: where it was from, how it was made and its variations. They told me they used mashed potatoes and other ingredients to make the teeny pillows of heaven. I really wanted to put them in this book, but I needed a quicker method, so I threw tradition to the wind and made up my own version with flour and mascarpone, drawing on British dumplings for inspiration. They are great to make in bulk and freeze raw. Also try experimenting with other sauces, such as the all'arrabbiata on page 156.

+ First, prepare the pesto. Finely grate the Parmesan and tip it into a blender or food processor. Peel the garlic, tear the leaves from the basil and add both with the oil and pine nuts. Blitz to a paste, season and set aside.

+ Now, for the gnocchi. Finely grate the Parmesan and tip it into a medium bowl. Pick the thyme leaves and add them (or the oregano) with the mascarpone, flour, eggs and salt and pepper. Mix to give a soft dough. Tip it onto a lightly floured surface and knead to form a smooth ball.

+ Divide the mixture into three and roll each out into a sausage about 60cm long. Cut each into 2cm pieces to give about 30 (90 in total). Halfway through, put two large frying pans each on a medium to high heat with a drizzle of oil and knob of the butter. Divide the gnocchi between the two pans and turn the heat down low. Leave the gnocchi to cook on one side for a minute, then carefully turn them over with a fish slice. Cook for 4 minutes more, continuing to turn them every so often until they are crisp and golden all over and warmed through. If all the gnocchi didn't fit in your pans then tip the cooked ones in a bowl, cover with tin foil to keep warm and cook the remainder adding more oil and butter as necessary.

+ Once all the gnocchi are cooked, toss the pesto and rocket through until evenly coated. Then, divide them among four plates. Scatter the pine nuts over. Add a good squeeze of lemon juice, a grind of pepper and serve.

Cakes + puds

'Everything in moderation … including moderation.'
Julia Child

For me, my life is not complete without the occasional
bit of cake or pud: soft, squidgy chocolate cake, no-
bake cheesecake or a citrusy, crunchy lemon and lime
drizzle cake. There is nothing quite like that moment
when a cake or dessert (made with such care and
attention) is brought to the table to awaiting mouths,
to be met with oooooohs and ahhhhhs and doesn't
that look lovelys. Making cakes for me is cathartic —
watching the eggs, sugar, flour and other such basic
ingredients combine together to create something
that usually becomes the sparkling jewel in the entire
meal's crown.

Prep time: **15 minutes**
Chilling time: **10 minutes in the freezer (or 20 minutes in the fridge)**
Time baking in the oven:
25 minutes
Makes: **8 pies**
Equipment: **Large baking sheet, medium bowl (if using shop-bought apple sauce), zester, rolling pin, pastry brush, sieve**

800g Bramley apple sauce (see page 295 if making yourself, but shop-bought is fine too)

If using shop-bought apple sauce

1 lemon

1 tsp ground cinnamon

1 tsp ground ginger

Pastry

Small handful of plain flour

500g puff pastry (shop-bought, or to make your own see page 266)

1 medium egg

Icing sugar, for dusting

Softly whipped cream, ice cream or crème anglaise (see page 292), to serve

Little warm Bramley apple pies or 'chaussons aux pommes'

Shop-bought apple sauce is fine to use. In fact it is a great time saver when in a hurry; ditto for the pastry. There may be some leftover pastry here, which can be wrapped up and frozen and kept for a month. Or roll it out into a rectangle, spread on either tapenade or chopped sundried tomatoes, roll up like a Swiss roll, then slice in 1cm slices and bake. Hey presto — easy little canapés.

+ Line a large baking sheet with baking parchment and set aside.

+ If you are using shop-bought apple sauce, just empty it into a medium bowl and finely grate the lemon zest over. Add the cinnamon and ginger, stir everything well to combine and set aside. If using your own homemade apple sauce, make sure it is completely cool before using (and simply skip to the next step).

+ Put some flour on the work surface and roll the pastry out to a 40cm square. Keep the pastry moving around as you roll so it does not stick, adding more flour underneath if need be. The pastry will be really nice and thin. Then cut out eight 10 x 20cm rectangles (cut the pastry in half and then across the opposite way into quarters) and arrange them on the baking sheet.

+ Crack the egg into a mug, whisk it lightly and then, using a pastry brush, brush a 1cm border around the edge of each pastry rectangle (and hang on to the remaining egg for later). Then, using up all of the apple sauce, put a few dollops of it on one half of each one (inside the border). Stuff as much of the apple sauce as you can inside the pastries otherwise they won't look nice and plump when they're cooked. Fold the other half of the pastry over the apple and use your fingers to press the edges down to seal. Press in good and tight to the apple so everything is nice and cosy.

>

Little warm Bramley apple pies or 'chaussons aux pommes'

+ Put the pies in the freezer for 10 minutes to firm up (or the fridge will do just fine if you have double that time to spare). Preheat the oven to 200°C, (fan 180°C), 400°F, Gas Mark 6.

+ Once firm, remove them from the freezer, brush liberally with the remaining egg and then mark the top of the pastries with a sharp knife with whatever pattern you like. I like to do the outline of an apple. Put them in the oven for about 25 minutes.

+ Once cooked the pastry should be crisp and golden brown, so remove the pies from the oven. Leave to cool a bit before eating (that apple gets super hot!). I really love to eat these while they are nice and warm, but they are very tasty served cool too. Either way, give a sift of icing sugar over them before tucking in with a little softly whipped cream, ice cream or crème anglaise.

40 minutes

Serves: **4**

Equipment: **Large roasting tin, zester, small frying pan, pestle and mortar (or mug and rolling pin), small bowl, sieve**

---

4 ripe peaches or nectarines

4 fresh figs

2 ripe pears

250ml dark rum (or port or apple juice for something non-alcoholic)

3 tbsp soft light brown sugar

1 vanilla pod (or vanilla extract)

1 cinnamon stick

2 sprigs of fresh rosemary

1 orange

To serve

Handful (about 25g) of toasted hazelnuts (they come ready toasted from the supermarket)

250g half- or full-fat crème fraîche

50g icing sugar

Whole nutmeg

Rum punch roast pears, figs & peaches with toasted hazelnuts & vanilla crème fraîche

This recipe has all sorts of parts to it which reflect my heritage and what I am about. The rum punch is a gentle nod to my Caribbean Island girl roots and the peaches and pears point to the fact that a huge part of me is quintessentially English.

+ Preheat the oven to 200°C, (fan 180°C), 400°F, Gas Mark 6.

+ Halve the peaches or nectarines and discard the stones, halve or quarter the figs, depending on size, and then quarter the pears lengthways and remove their cores. Arrange all of the fruit pieces, cut side up, in a large roasting tin.

+ Next drizzle over the rum (or port or apple juice) and scatter the sugar over. Use a sharp knife to split the vanilla pod in half lengthways and add half of the pod to the fruit, reserving the other half for later (or add a couple of drops of vanilla extract, if preferred).

+ Snap the cinnamon stick in half and throw it in with the leaves from the rosemary sprigs. Finely grate the zest of the orange all over the fruits, then halve it and squeeze the juice over also.

+ Cover the tin tightly with tin foil and roast in the oven for 30 minutes, removing the foil after 20 minutes (and giving the fruit a quick baste with the juices before putting it back in).

+ Spoon the crème fraîche into a small bowl and sift the icing sugar over. Scrape the vanilla seeds from the reserved half of the vanilla pod and add them too (or a couple of drops of vanilla extract). Stir everything together to just combine.

>

Rum punch roast pears, figs & peaches with toasted hazelnuts & vanilla crème fraîche

(continued)

+ Remove the fruit from the oven once cooked. It should be deliciously soft and sticky and the sauce rich and syrupy.

+ Spoon the fruits out onto warmed serving plates. Each person will have two peach halves, two or four fig pieces, depending on how they were cut, and two pieces of pear. Dollop some crème fraîche to the side, add a sprinkling of toasted hazelnuts, finely grate a little nutmeg over the top and serve.

Time from start to finish:
10 minutes (if using shop-bought meringues. See next page for homemade)
Serves: 6
Equipment: Large bowl and hand whisk or hand-held electric whisk or freestanding electric mixer set with the whisk attachment, small bowl and microwave (or small pan) (optional)

1 stem ginger ball (this comes in syrup and can be found in the baking section of the supermarket)

½ vanilla pod (or a couple of drops of vanilla extract)

300ml whipping or double cream (keep it in the fridge until you need it so it whips up more easily)

50g icing sugar

12 meringue nests (shop-bought, or for homemade see page 225)

300g blackberries

50g white or dark chocolate, to drizzle (optional)

A few fresh mint leaves, to serve

Neat-and-tidy Eton mess with blackberries & stem ginger whipped cream

There are times when I feel that the kitchen is my haven and wild horses could not drag me away from it. It is then that I make these white, crispy cradles from scratch. At other times (which, if you are like me, seem to occur far to often these days), then I am dashing around the kitchen to pull off a pudding in 20 minutes flat. So I have given the choice of both to alternate at your will. And the fruit and cream spiked with peppery ginger is almost good enough to eat on its own!

+ If you are using shop-bought meringues then carry straight on with the recipe. If you are going to make the meringues from scratch then turn over the page for the recipe and whilst they are cooking turn back to this page to make the filling.

+ Finely chop the stem ginger ball and then split the piece of vanilla pod open and remove the seeds. Set both aside.

+ Pour the cream into a large bowl and sift in the icing sugar. Whip it up until it just begins to go thick. A hand-held or freestanding electric whisk or a food mixer makes light work of this, but you can do this with a hand whisk and plenty of elbow grease.

+ Gently stir the ginger and vanilla seeds (or extract, if using) through with as few stirs as possible.

+ Arrange six of the meringues on a large serving platter or cake stand and, using half the cream, put a blob on each one. Arrange the blackberries on the cream, and then use the rest of the cream up on top. Sit the remaining meringues on top, pretty side up.

+ For something really fancy, melt the white or dark chocolate in a small bowl either in 30-second blasts in a microwave or set over a small pan of simmering water. Use a small spoon or fork to drizzle it back and forth across the meringue stacks. Rip over some mint leaves and serve.

Prep time: **20 minutes**
Time baking in the oven:
30–40 minutes
Cooling time: **20–30 minutes**
Makes: **12 meringues**
Equipment: **8cm saucer or
bowl, 2 large baking sheets,
medium bowl and hand whisk
or hand-held electric whisk
(or freestanding electric mixer
set with the whisk attachment),
piping bag fitted with 2D or star
nozzle (optional)**

4 medium egg whites (at room
temperature) or125ml pasteurised egg
whites (I found them in the milk section
of the supermarket)

Squeeze of lemon juice

225g caster sugar

1 tsp cornflour

Homemade meringues

This is my failsafe meringue recipe, used here for these
little nests. This works well for a pavlova too or for the
meringue on top of a lemon meringue pie. You could try
something different and stir in a couple of handfuls of
roasted chopped hazelnuts to add crunch.

+ Preheat the oven to 130°C, (fan 110°C), 250°F, Gas Mark ½. Using
  an 8cm-diameter template (like a saucer or bowl), mark out 12 circles on
  2 sheets of baking parchment. Turn them face down onto 2 large baking
  sheets and set aside.

+ Now for the meringues. Get a really clean medium bowl. If it is not
  spotlessly clean, it can mean that the egg whites don't whip up properly.
  This goes for all the equipment.

+ A hand-held electric whisk or freestanding electric mixer is best for the
  job, but you can do this with a hand whisk and plenty of elbow grease.
  Tip the egg whites into the bowl, squeeze the lemon juice in and then
  whisk them to a medium peak. To test, lift the whisk out of the meringue
  with some of the white foam on the end. Then point it upwards and the
  bit of meringue on the end should flop over like Noddy's floppy red hat.

+ Next add a spoonful of the sugar to the meringue and whisk really hard
  until all of the sugar has 'dissolved' and the mixture starts to look a bit
  shiny. Then add the remaining sugar gradually, while whisking all the
  time, until the mixture becomes really shiny and very stiff.

+ If you perform the whisk trick at this time, the peak would be almost
  straight up in the air with only a hint of Noddy's floppy red hat. If you are
  using egg white from a carton, the peak will still remain quite floppy, but
  the mixture will be very shiny and stiff.

+ Finally, whisk in the cornflour for a second or two until smooth. This gives
  the meringue a bit of an inner chewiness.

>

Chocolate mousse
with raspberries

(continued)

+ Once the whites are lovely and thick and glossy, stir in a spoonful of the chocolate mixture. This will loosen the whites up a bit and make it easier to manage the next step. Gradually pour all of the chocolate into the egg whites and then gently fold them together. Try not to be too heavy-handed or over mix this, as it is good to keep as much air as possible in it.

+ Divide between the four 150ml glasses or ramekins and lightly press the raspberries into the tops. Cover each one loosely with cling film and then pop in the fridge for 30 minutes or so to firm up (or if you want to eat them ASAP, put them in the freezer for 15 minutes). These can be made in the morning for a dinner party in the evening. If in the fridge for that long, I like to take them out 15 minutes or so before I need them so that they are not too cold for the guests.

+ Just before serving, decorate the top of the mousse with icing sugar. I hold a piece of paper with a straight edge quite closely over the part I don't want the icing sugar to be on and then dust away (through a fine sieve) to give a nice detail over about a third of the top.

Cakes + puds

Strawberry & cream mini cakes with chocolate drizzle strawberries

Prep time: **15 minutes, plus 5 minutes if using the sugar syrup**
Time baking in the oven:
25 minutes
Cooling and assembly time:
25 minutes
Makes: **12 mini cakes**
Equipment: **12-hole muffin tin, 12 muffin/cupcake paper cases, large bowl, mechanical ice cream scoop (optional), small pan (if making sugar syrup), large wire rack, pastry brush (optional), small bowl, large bowl, fine sieve, hand whisk, small bowl and microwave or medium pan**

Sponge

250g soft salted butter

250g caster sugar

5 medium eggs (at room temperature)

250g self-raising flour

1 tsp baking powder

Pinch of salt

½ vanilla pod (or a couple of drops of vanilla extract)

Sugar syrup (optional)

100g granulated or caster sugar

100ml water

Filling

300ml whipping or double cream

50g icing sugar

½ vanilla pod (or a couple of drops of vanilla extract)

To assemble

175g good strawberry jam

75g white chocolate, for drizzling

12 strawberries preferably with a little bit of stem attached (but stemless is fine too)

On the show, I am always making things in my kitchen mixer. Someone pointed out that not everyone has a kitchen mixer and would I mind writing the recipe for people who make it by hand. So here it is. Among other things, the secret to a good cake is to make sure the ingredients are all at room temperature. If your eggs are fridge cold, put them in a bowl filled with warm water for a few minutes to warm them up a bit. I like my cakes to be really moist so I've included a recipe for sugar syrup. This is optional, though, and the cakes will taste just fine without it if you choose not to include this step.

+ Preheat the oven to 180°C, (fan 160°C), 350°F, Gas Mark 4. Line the 12-hole muffin tin with paper cases and set aside.

+ First, get started on the sponge. Put the butter in a large bowl. If it is not soft, then either grate it in or get your hands in and really squidge and squeeze it for a moment or two. Messy? Yes. Fun? Absolutely!

+ When the butter is soft add the sugar. Use a wooden spoon to really beat it all together well. It won't go that fluffy by hand, but it will go a bit lighter and everything should be very soft.

+ Add the eggs (I admit I just chuck them all in at once) and then beat the whole thing like mad for a couple of minutes until it all combines. The strength of your beating will ensure that everything comes together nicely. Now add in the flour, baking powder and salt. Split the vanilla pod open with a small knife, scrape the seeds out of one half and add them too (or the vanilla extract, if using). Then mix everything together so it is just combined.

>

Strawberry & cream mini cakes with chocolate drizzle strawberries

(continued)

+ Now, using two spoons (or a mechanical ice cream scoop if you have one), divide the mixture between the 12 cases and then put them into the oven to bake for 25 minutes.

+ If you've decided to use the sugar syrup for extra-moist cakes, then make it now. Put the sugar in a small pan with 100ml of cold water and place on a medium heat. Allow the sugar to dissolve, stirring from time to time. Then, once the sugar has dissolved, whack up the heat and boil it for 2 minutes before removing and setting aside.

+ To tell if the sponges are cooked, they should spring back when touched and be a rich golden brown. Remove them from the oven and leave to cool in the tin for a few minutes until cool enough to handle.

+ Remove their paper cases and cut the cakes in half across the equator. Arrange the bottoms and tops, cut side up but separately from each other, on a large cooling rack. This will also help them to cool down completely much more quickly. If you are using the (optional) sugar syrup, then brush the cakes liberally with it as soon as they have been cut in half.

+ Once they are almost cool, prepare everything for assembly. Spoon the strawberry jam into a small bowl, give it a good stir to loosen it up and set aside.

+ Next put the cream into a large bowl and sift the icing sugar in. Scrape the seeds out of the other half of the vanilla pod and add them too (or the vanilla extract, if using). Whisk it up until it just begins to thicken and then set it aside.

+ Now, melt the white chocolate for drizzling. Break up the chocolate and put it in a small bowl. Melt it in the microwave in 30-second blasts, stirring between each addition. Otherwise, put the bowl over a pan of simmering water, making sure that the bottom of the bowl does not touch the water as this can make the chocolate go grainy and lumpy.

+ Assemble once the cakes are completely cool. Put a dollop of strawberry jam on each of the cake bottoms, followed by a dollop of the cream. Put the other halves on top and then put another dollop of the cream on the top of that. Place an unhulled strawberry on each mini cake. Finally, use a fork to drizzle the melted white chocolate over.

+ Arrange on a large platter or cake stand or lift straight onto small plates and serve.

Prep time: 20 minutes (if using ready-rolled pastry)
Time baking in the oven: 35–45 minutes
Serves: 6
Equipment: 10 x 34cm fluted loose-bottomed flan tin (at least 2.5cm deep), rolling pin, baking sheet, medium bowl and hand-held electric whisk (or freestanding electric mixer fitted with the paddle attachment), colander, small bowl, fine sieve

Pastry

375g pack of ready-rolled dessert pastry

or

500g pack of shortcrust pastry

or

500g homemade sweet shortcrust pastry (see page 269)

Almond filling

100g soft butter

100g caster sugar

100g ground almonds

3 tbsp plain flour, plus a little extra for dusting

1 medium egg

1 tbsp amaretto liqueur

Topping

411g tin of pear halves or 4 very ripe soft pears

Cream

250g tub of mascarpone

1 stem ginger ball (the type in syrup)

½ vanilla pod (or a couple of drops of vanilla extract)

50g icing sugar

To serve

1 tsp icing sugar

Small handful of fresh mint

Pear, almond & amaretto tart with stem ginger mascarpone cream

I have had my eye on this little tart for some time. I first consumed one like this in all its ambrosial splendour in a supermarket café in France. Determined to recreate one like it at home, I set about trying to make it from memory. Being challenged many times over to find pears in the peak of their ripeness, a can of their tinned counterparts came to the rescue with very pleasing results.

+ Preheat the oven to 180°C, (fan 160°C), 350°F, Gas Mark 4.

+ Unravel the ready-rolled pastry (if using) and use it to line the flan tin. Roll it out a touch more, if necessary, to fit in perfectly. If using a block of shop-bought or ball of homemade pastry, then roll out to just bigger than the tin on a floured surface and use in the same way. Either way, be really careful to not stretch the pastry or pull it, as this will make it shrink in the tin when it cooks.

+ Try and get the pastry right into the fluted edges of the tin. I use a wooden spoon handle dipped in some flour to ease the pastry into the 'flutes'. Cut off the excess pastry with a sharp knife and then sit the tin on a baking sheet and pop in the fridge to harden up a bit while you prepare the filling.

+ Mix the butter and sugar together in a medium bowl either by hand or using a hand-held electric whisk (or in a freestanding electric mixer) until it is really soft and well combined. Then beat in the ground almonds and plain flour. Crack the egg in, add the amaretto liqueur, and then beat it hard so everything is combined. Remove the lined tin from the fridge and add the almond filling, spreading it out evenly so it is nice and smooth on top.

>

Pear, almond
& amaretto tart
with stem ginger
mascarpone cream

(continued)

+ Drain the tinned pears well in a colander and then on kitchen paper. Or peel, halve and decore the fresh pears, if using.

+ Arrange the pear halves, cut side down, in the almond filling. If you lay the tin running from left to right in front of you, then lay a pear half in pointing away from you, then the next one pointing towards you and so on, so they are in an alternating pattern and all fit in perfectly.

+ Bake in the oven for 35–45 minutes or until the filling is nicely puffed up and golden.

+ About 5 minutes before the tart is ready, put the mascarpone in a small bowl. Finely chop the stem ginger, split the vanilla pod open and scrape out the seeds and add them (or the vanilla extract, if using) to the bowl. Sift the icing sugar in and then stir everything together gently. Just give it a few stirs or otherwise the mascarpone may split and go grainy. Set aside for serving.

+ Check the tart is cooked. The pastry will be crisp and golden and the almond filling should have puffed up a little around the pears and be golden brown and spongy. Stick a skewer or point of a sharp knife into the centre of the filling to check it is done. It will be just a little damp from the moisture of the pears, but shouldn't be really wet like the original raw mixture.

+ Once cooked, remove from the oven and leave to cool in the tin for a few minutes before carefully removing it from the tin. I sit the tin on two upturned glasses and drop the side of the tin down to reveal the tart. Then simply slide the tart off the base onto a long serving platter.

+ To decorate, hold the base of the tin quite close to the tart to cover all but about 2cm of one of the long edges. Then dust half of the icing sugar over through a fine sieve. Repeat with the other long edge. Sprinkle over some picked mint leaves and serve warm with the ginger mascarpone cream. This is also really good served cold.

Prep time: **20 minutes**
Chilling time: **30 minutes in the freezer (or 4 hours in the fridge)**
Serves: **12**
Equipment: **Large pan, plastic food bag and rolling pin (or food processor), 23cm springform tin (at least 8cm deep), 2 large bowls, zester, fine sieve, hand–held electric whisk (optional), offset spatula (optional)**

75g butter

250g digestive biscuits

2 tbsp soft light brown sugar

800g full-fat cream cheese (half-fat just does not hold)

1 lemon

1 vanilla pod (or a couple of drops of vanilla extract)

800ml fridge-cold double cream

75g icing sugar

Doorstop vanilla cheesecake

This is my ultimate vanilla cheesecake. It's not too sweet, but if you prefer it sweeter then 50g extra icing sugar should do the trick, but taste it before it goes into the tin to make sure you're happy. The lemon zest gives it a nice freshness without necessarily tasting lemony. If you want a lemony edge to it, simply add the zest of one or two more lemons, again tasting it before using.

+ Put the butter in a large pan over a low heat and leave to melt. Place the digestive biscuits in a plastic food bag, seal it up and bash them with a rolling pin to give fine crumbs. It's also quicker and easier to blitz them in a food processor if you have one.

+ Tip the crushed biscuits into the now-melted butter, add the soft light brown sugar and mix together well. Then evenly squidge the mixture into the bottom of the cake tin, really packing it in tight by pressing it down with your hand or the back of a spoon. Place in the fridge to firm up while you make the topping.

+ Put the cream cheese in a large bowl and finely grate the zest over. Halve the vanilla pod, scrape out the seeds and add them (or the vanilla extract) too. Mix together well to loosen the mixture slightly.

+ Pour the double cream into a large bowl and sift in the icing sugar. Whisk it, by hand or with a hand-held electric whisk, to almost the same consistency as the cream cheese, just a little looser.

+ Then tip the cream into the cream cheese mixture and mix everything gently, with as few stirs as possible. Tip it onto the biscuit base and smooth the top with the back of a spoon or an offset spatula.

+ Cover with cling film and put it in the freezer for about 30 minutes until just set. You can of course set this in the fridge, but it will take

>

Doorstop vanilla cheesecake

(continued)

considerably longer (about 4 hours). Handy to know if making in advance, though obviously you wouldn't want to leave it in the freezer for too long!

+ Remove the cheesecake from the fridge/freezer 10 minutes or so before serving to bring to room temperature a bit (but don't leave it out for too long as it will go too soft).

+ Serve and enjoy, enjoy, enjoy.

Prep time: **30 minutes**
Time baking in the oven:
35–45 minutes
Makes: **9 big squares or
12 small ones**
Equipment: **20cm-square
cake tin, small pan, baking
tray (optional), large bowl and
hand-held electric whisk (or
freestanding electric mixer fitted
with the whisk attachment),
large flat plate**

Sticky topping

50g butter, plus extra for greasing

50g soft light brown sugar

Sponge

Handful of pecan nuts (about 50g)
(optional)

150g soft butter

175g soft light brown

4 medium eggs (at room temperature)

½ vanilla pod (or a couple of drops of
vanilla extract)

100g self-raising flour

75g wholemeal flour

1 tsp baking powder

3 tsp ground ginger

1 tsp ground cinnamon

1 tbsp treacle

Pinch of salt

Bananas

2 small, firm bananas

1 tbsp Calvados (optional)

To serve

Crème anglaise (see page 292) or
softly whipped cream or ice cream

Dulce & banana cake

A super-quick, super-tasty banana tray bake. I am
sure most of you know that dulce is Italian for 'sweet'.
I came up with this one night sitting in front of the telly
half-watching TV. I thought of my old job in fashion,
I thought of a famous Italian design duo and, well, then
I thought up the name of this cake!

+ Preheat the oven to 180°C, (fan 160°C), 350°F, Gas Mark 4, with
the middle shelf at the ready. Grease and line the cake tin with baking
parchment and grease again.

+ First, make the sticky topping. Place the butter and soft light brown sugar
in a small pan over a medium heat. Once the butter is melted, turn up the
heat and let the mixture bubble away for a few minutes until it begins to
thicken slightly. Stir it frequently so it does not catch on the bottom. Pour
the mixture into the bottom of the lined tin and tip the tin back and forth to
spread it out evenly (the mixture will eventually solidify in the tin so make
sure to spread it out now).

+ Next, tip the pecans (if using) onto a baking tray and toast in the oven
for 5 minutes. Remove the pecan nuts from the oven once toasted and set
aside to cool.

+ Now, make the sponge mixture. Cream together the butter and the
sugar in a large bowl, by hand or with a hand-held electric whisk (or
freestanding electric mixer) until it becomes a little lighter in colour. Then
add the eggs one at time, beating hard between each addition. Split
the vanilla pod open, scrape the seeds out and add (or add the vanilla
extract). Then fold in both flours, the baking powder, ginger, cinnamon,
treacle and salt and set aside.

+ Take the bananas and slice them into 5mm thick pieces. Arrange them
in a single layer in the bottom of the tin. I line them up so they are nice
and straight, but of course it is fine to do them in any old order too. Pack
them all in tight so they don't move around once the cake mix goes over.
Drizzle over the Calvados, if using.

>

Dulce & banana cake
(continued)

+ Roughly chop the pecan nuts and stir them through the cake mix. Now carefully dollop the cake mix over the bananas and gently spread it out with the back of a spoon or with a palette knife, levelling the top. Then pop it into the oven for about 35–45 minutes or so to cook.

+ After the cake has been cooking for 35 minutes, remove it from the oven and insert a metal skewer or the blade of a small knife right into the centre (but not touching the bottom). It should come out completely clean. If there is some cakey gooeyness left on it, just pop the tin back in the oven for another 5 minutes or so.

+ Once the cake is cooked, remove it from the oven and leave to cool in the tin for about 10 minutes. Then put a large flat plate over the top of the tin and, holding the tin and the plate, flip the whole lot over so that the tin is now upside down. Gently remove the tin and peel off the baking parchment to reveal your very tasty dulce and banana underneath!

+ Cut into squares and serve warm or cold with your choice of crème anglaise, softly whipped cream or ice cream. Salted Caramel Toffee Sauce also goes a treat with this (see page 294) or even a shop-bought one if you fancy.

Prep time: **25 minutes**
Time baking in the oven:
approx 25 minutes
Serves: **8**
Equipment: **Kettle, 2 x 20cm
loose-bottomed sandwich tins,
large baking sheet, mug, 2 large
bowls, pastry brush, wire rack,
fine sieve**

Sponge

175g very soft butter, plus extra for
greasing

1–3 tbsp instant coffee powder

100g walnut halves

150g self-raising flour

50g wholemeal flour

200g soft light brown sugar

1 tsp baking powder

4 medium eggs (at room temperature)

1 tsp vanilla extract

Coffee syrup

1 tsp instant coffee powder

1 tbsp caster sugar

Buttercream

100g icing sugar

200g very soft butter

2 tbsp instant coffee powder

Simply coffee, vanilla & walnut cake

One of the first cakes I ever ate was a simple coffee cake. No bells, no whistles, nothing fancy, simply coffee cake with a rich coffee buttercream. I have, however, played around with the recipe a bit and added 50g of wholemeal flour, which gives a tasty, nutty dimension to the sponge. But if you don't have wholemeal flour in the cupboard, then just make this up with 50g of plain flour instead for an equally appetising cake.

+ Preheat the oven to 180°C, (fan 160°C), 350°F, Gas Mark 4, and put the kettle on to boil (with just a small amount of water in). Grease the bottom of the sandwich tins with butter and line with baking parchment. Sit them on a large baking sheet and set aside.

+ First make the sponge. Put the coffee powder into a mug, using 1 tablespoon for a subtle coffee flavour or 3 tablespoons if you want to be awake for quite some time! For me, 3 is just right. Then add 1 tablespoon of hot water from the kettle for every tablespoon of coffee and mix until smooth. Finely chop half of the walnuts and set aside.

+ Put the flours into a large bowl along with the sugar and baking powder and mix a bit to combine. Then add the butter, eggs, vanilla extract, prepared coffee and chopped walnuts (reserving the halves for decoration). Beat it hard until smooth and well combined. Divide the mixture evenly between the two tins and then pop them in the oven for around 25 minutes.

+ About 5 minutes before the cake is ready, put the kettle on again for the coffee syrup. Spoon the coffee powder into the mug with the sugar and 2 tablespoons of hot water from the kettle. Stir until the sugar has dissolved and set aside.

>

Simply coffee, vanilla & walnut cake

(continued)

+ Check the cakes are ready. A skewer inserted in the middle should come out clean. Return to the oven for another 5 or so minutes if not. Once ready, remove from the oven and brush liberally with the coffee sugar syrup to give a wonderfully soft sponge. Then leave the cakes to cool for a few minutes until cool enough to handle. Carefully remove from the tins, peel off the paper and leave to cool completely on a wire rack.

+ Cooling should take about 10 minutes so, as they cool, make the buttercream. Sift the icing sugar into a large bowl. Add the butter and beat hard until light and fluffy. Blend the coffee powder in the mug with 1 tablespoon of hot water from the kettle and stir into the buttercream.

+ Once the sponges have cooled, put one on a cake stand or serving plate and slather the top liberally with half of the buttercream. It will be a good thick layer. Place the other sponge on top and slather the remaining buttercream over. Arrange the remaining walnuts on top. Totally yum.

Prep time: 20 minutes
Time baking in the oven:
30–40 minutes
Serves: 6 (two slices each)
Equipment: 450g loaf tin, large
bowl and hand–held electric
whisk (or freestanding electric
mixer), zester, small bowl,
wire rack

125g soft butter, plus a little extra for greasing

150g caster sugar

½ vanilla pod (or a couple of drops of vanilla extract)

3 medium eggs (at room temperature)

150g self-raising flour

1 tsp baking powder

Pinch of salt

1 lemon

1 lime

4 tbsp poppy seeds

50g icing sugar

Lemon & lime poppy seed drizzle cake

I have made lemon drizzle cake a gazillion times and love it, but I do like to add a twist to recipes. So while tidying up my spice rack, I found a jar of poppy seeds alone in the corner, which had been untouched for some time. I was inspired to throw these into my lemon drizzle mix with some lime for good measure. The resulting cake was a resounding success; the family dived in moments after it surfaced from the oven.

ı Preheat the oven to 180°C, (fan 160°C), 350°F, Gas Mark 4, with the middle shelf at the ready. Grease and line the loaf tin with baking parchment and grease again. I don't usually line all the sides, but I use a strip that sits into the tin lengthways and leaves a little overhang at either end. This makes it much easier to pull the cake from the tin once cooked.

+ Cream the butter and sugar together in a large bowl with a hand-held electric whisk (or using a freestanding electric mixer) until light and fluffy. Then split open the vanilla pod, scrape out the seeds and add them (or the vanilla extract) with 2 of the eggs and beat like mad again.

+ The mixture may look less than perfect at this stage, but keep going and it will come good. Add the last egg and beat like mad, then add in the flour, baking powder and salt and finely grate in the lemon and lime zests. Stir the poppy seeds through, then tip the whole lot into the loaf tin. Spread the mixture flat with the back of a spoon and bake for 35 minutes.

+ Meanwhile, put the icing sugar in a small bowl. Squeeze in about 1 tablespoon of juice from either the lemon or lime. Add enough to give a runny drizzle, stirring between each addition, and then set this aside.

+ Check the cake after 30 minutes to see if it is cooked. Insert a skewer or the blade of a small knife into the centre of the cake. It should come out clean. If not, pop it back into the oven for another 5 minutes or so. Once cooked, leave it to cool for a few minutes in the tin. Pull it out using the paper, then peel it off and transfer to a wire rack until cool. Place it on a serving plate, drizzle the drizzle over the top, slice into 12 and serve!

Prep time: **15 minutes**, plus 25 minutes to cool and 20 minutes to decorate
Time baking in the oven: **25–30 minutes**
Serves: **8–10**
Equipment: **2 x 20cm loose-bottomed sandwich tins, large baking sheet, large bowl and hand-held electric whisk (or freestanding electric mixer), wire rack, medium bowl and microwave or medium pan, fine sieve**

Sponge

150g really soft butter, plus a little extra for greasing

250g caster sugar

150g self-raising flour

125g sour cream

4 medium eggs (at room temperature)

50g cocoa powder

1 tsp baking powder

Pinch of salt

½ vanilla pod (or a couple of drops of vanilla extract)

Buttercream

100g dark chocolate (minimum 70% cocoa solids)

550g icing sugar

250g really soft butter

2 tbsp milk (or water)

To decorate

4 x 135g packets of brown or white Maltesers

Let them eat cake, cake

The other day my daughter and I were messing around with some M&M's and we stuck them all over a cake. It looked very cool, but was not really very 'me'. So we both racked our brains and came up with Maltesers as a worthy substitute! This cake is one of those 'faster' cakes, rather than 'fast', but the all-in-one sponge is a bung-it-all-in-and-go method, which makes things a lot easier. The great thing that is not the quickest is sticking on the Malteser balls, but give your child (or a willing adult) the Maltesers and let them stick the little balls on to their heart's content.

+ Preheat the oven to 180°C, (fan 160°C), 350°F, Gas Mark 4, with the middle shelf at the ready. Grease the sandwich tins with a little butter, line the bottoms with discs of baking parchment and sit them on a large baking sheet.

+ Put the butter, sugar, flour, sour cream, eggs, cocoa powder, baking powder and salt in a large bowl or in a freestanding electric mixer or a food processor. Split the vanilla pod open, scrape out the seeds and add them also (or the vanilla extract). Then mix or blend to give a smooth, soft mixture.

+ Divide evenly between the cake tins, smooth the tops and place in the oven for 25–30 minutes.

+ To check the cakes are baked, insert a skewer into the middle of each cake and if it comes out clean, then they are ready to come out. Remove them from the oven and leave to cool in the tins for a few minutes before carefully removing and leaving to cool completely on a wire rack (about 25 minutes).

+ When the cakes are almost cool, start making the buttercream. Break the chocolate into a medium bowl and melt it in the microwave in 30-second blasts, stirring between each blast. Otherwise, sit the bowl of chocolate on a medium pan of simmering water, making sure that the water does not touch the bottom of the bowl (as this may make the chocolate grainy).

>

Crouching tiger, hidden zebra cake

(continued)

+ Check the cake is cooked by inserting a skewer into the centre. It should come out clean. If not, then return to the oven for another 5 minutes or so until cooked. Once cooked, remove from the oven and allow to cool for a few minutes in the tin. Then carefully remove from the tin and leave to cool completely on a wire rack (but it is also fine to eat it warm!).

+ Cut the cake into six wedges to reveal its spongy gold. Arrange on a cake stand or platter and serve.

Bread + pastry

'Food for the body is not enough.
There must be food for the soul as well.'
Dorothy Day

I am truly, madly, deeply passionate about bread.
I don't just mean I am in love with eating the entire
bread basket every time I go out for a meal, with
lashings of the butter that accompanies it, I mean the
making of it. There are days when I feel on top of the
world and days when the world feels like it has all its
weight on me, but often I will throw some flour and the
other necessary ingredients into a bowl and use the
making of the dough as a mode of therapy to get me
out of my black dog blues. Kneading by hand releases
a multitude of angst and the smell of freshly baked
bread fills my head with happiness. Fresh home-baked
bread is instant culinary gratification at its finest.

Prep time: **15 minutes**
Time baking in the oven:
35 minutes
Makes: **1 loaf**
Equipment: **Large bowl, baking tray**

3 sprigs of fresh rosemary

75g pitted green or black olives

450g self-raising flour, plus extra for dusting

½ tsp salt

1 tbsp extra virgin olive oil

225ml cold water

Fruity olive oil and balsamic vinegar, to serve

Aussie olive damper bread (soda bread's antipodean cousin)

I first went to Sydney in my teens and when I saw the Opera House, I fell head over heels in love with the place. This is an Australian bread traditionally (I am led to believe) made by people in the bush on the camp fire. I love green olives, but the black variety, although normally a little more bitter, work well too.

+ Preheat the oven to 200°C, (fan 180°C), 400°F, Gas Mark 6 and put a baking tray in to warm up.

+ Pick the leaves from the rosemary and roughly chop them up. Roughly chop the olives also and set them aside in separate piles.

+ Put the flour in a large bowl with the rosemary, salt, oil and water. Mix everything well until the dough starts to come together in a ball. Then get your hands in and squidge all the dry bits in, using the bread like a cloth to gather the bits all up.

+ Dust a clean work surface with a little flour and place the dough down. Squish it into a flattish round, put the olives in the centre and squash them down a bit, bringing the edges of the dough towards the centre to cover the olives. Flip the dough over and knead the olives in. The dough may be quite wet with olives flying all over the shop, but just keep pushing the rogue olives back into the dough. If everything is too wet, add a small handful of flour. Shape it into a 20cm round and place on the warmed baking tray.

+ Rub a little flour onto the handle of a wooden spoon. Then, holding the handle horizontal to the bread, press down onto the loaf, making an indent almost to the bottom of the tray. Now turn the handle so that it is at a 90-degree angle to the first line and push down again to make a cross. Do this two more times so your bread looks like a kind of clock face of eight triangular portions.

+ Bake in the oven for 35 minutes or until the bread sounds hollow when tapped on the bottom. This is wonderful served warm with some fruity olive oil and balsamic vinegar.

Prep time: **10 minutes**
Proving time: **30–45 minutes**
Time baking in the oven:
25 minutes
Makes: **1 loaf**
Equipment: **Large bowl (or freestanding electric mixer set with the dough hook), baking sheet, small bowl**

Bread

400g strong white bread flour, plus extra for dusting

50g strong wholemeal bread flour

7g sachet of fast-action dried yeast

2 tsp salt

275ml water

A little sunflower oil (or oil spray)

Topping

25g rice flour (I found rice flour online from most supermarkets)

1 tsp caster sugar

¼ tsp fast-action dried yeast

Pinch of salt

1 tsp vegetable oil

1 tbsp warm water

Crackle-top bread

This is one of my cheeky recipes that I have slipped into the book under the guise of being fast(er) to prepare compared to using regular yeast and because there is also very little work to do. So a bit of slow stirring and kneading and that is basically it. Now, this little bread has caused some controversy recently over whether it looks like a giraffe or the tiger after which it is usually named, but for me, I prefer the US name 'Dutch crunch' or my own made-up name, crackle-top bread.

+ First, prepare the bread. Put the flours, yeast and salt into a large bowl (or food mixer) and give a quick mix to combine. Add 275ml of water, mixing all the time until everything comes together. Then get your hands in and squidge it into a ball. Add a couple more tablespoons of water if it's too dry. Knead it on a floured work surface for 10 minutes (or 5 minutes if using a food mixer).

+ To check to see if the dough has been kneaded enough, first make it into a ball with a taut top. Then put your finger in the flour and prod the side of the dough to make an indent. If the dough springs back all the way, then it is ready. If it only springs back a little, then knead it for a couple more minutes and try again.

+ Now flatten the bread ball out a little (to give a loaf roughly 5cm high by 12.5cm wide). Then pull the edges into the middle, making a little parcel type thing, and turn it over. This will give the dough a nice taut top. Cup the edges of the dough with your hands to shape it into a neat round shape and place on a baking sheet.

+ Oil some cling film and wrap it over the dough. Use several pieces if necessary so that it is completely covered, but not too tightly so there is room to rise. Put in a warm (but not too hot) place for 30–45 minutes or until it has increased in size by about 50 per cent.

+ Preheat the oven to 200°C, (fan 180°C), 400°F, Gas Mark 6 with the top shelf at the ready.

>

Twister bread

(continued)

a bundle and pick them all up in one go. Then twist them together so you have a long, thick, twisted rope made up of the individual strands of bread. Try to twist it evenly so the rope is an even thickness throughout.

+ Now curve the bread into a wreath shape and squish the ends together, sealing them with a bit of water. It does not have to be perfect, just as long as the ends are joined up. When I make this bread there are usually lots of poppy seeds left on the surface, so I scoop these up and then scatter them over the bread, especially the bit where the join is, to cover it up a bit.

+ Place the wreath on a baking sheet. Oil some cling film (I find the spray oil is best for this) and use it to cover the dough, oiled side down, so it is airtight but with enough room for the dough to rise a little.

+ I usually put the oven to preheat to 200°C, (fan 180°C), 400°F, Gas Mark 6 now and place the dough on a chair near it, so it's nice and warm. Leave to prove for about 30 minutes. To test if it is ready for the oven (because the bread will not have doubled in size, but probably grown by about half again), dust your finger with some flour and then make an indent in the side of the bread. The indent should spring back about halfway. If the indent just stays there and does not really move very much, then it needs more time.

+ When ready, place in the oven to bake for 35 minutes.

+ The loaf is cooked when it sounds hollow when tapped underneath. If not, then give it another 5 minutes or so in the oven.

+ Once ready, remove from the oven and serve. I love the crispy crunchy bits on the outside and the soft pillowy inside slathered in lots of butter.

Net bread (roti jala)

Time from start to finish:
20 minutes
Makes: **6 rotis**
Equipment: **Large jug, large frying pan (at least 30.5cm wide), piping bag fitted with a very small nozzle (about 3mm) or a disposable piping bag or squeezy bottle, baking tray**

125g plain flour
2 tsp curry powder
Pinch of salt
200ml coconut milk
1 medium egg
Vegetable oil

This Malaysian-inspired 'roti' looks suspiciously like my dear nan's favourite crocheted doily. I find the combination of coconut milk and curry powder a little bit addictive and make these to accompany anything a bit spicy with lots of sauce. Just fold up the rotis and mop up the juices. It's also delicious with some homemade Mango Chutney (see page 293). Very, very tasty.

+ Preheat the oven to 110°C, (fan 90°C), 225°F, Gas Mark ½.

+ Put the flour, curry powder and salt into a large jug and make a well in the centre. Gradually add the coconut milk, stirring all the time. Once all of the coconut milk is added, beat it hard to get rid of any lumps. Then crack the egg in, beat again and set aside.

+ Pour a tiny bit of oil into a large frying pan on a medium to high heat.

+ Pour the mixture into the piping bag fitted with a 3mm (approx) nozzle, or if you are using a disposable piping bag, simply snip enough from the tip of the bag to give a very small hole about 3mm wide. As the mixture is fairly runny, you will need to press the nozzle opening of the bag closed so it doesn't flow out as you fill it. Alternatively, you can use a squeezy bottle for this. You may need to snip a little off the bottle tip to make the opening ever so slightly bigger. It's a bit messy filling it up, but will still produce lovely rotis!

+ Once the pan is nice and hot, drizzle the mixture onto it in a loop-the-loop pattern, up and down the pan until all is covered. Make sure that all of the rows join up together so that the 'net' will hold once it is cooked.

+ Leave to cook for about 3 minutes or until the underside is just beginning to go a golden brown. Then carefully flip it over (as you would a pancake) and cook the other side for a couple of minutes.

+ Once the bread is cooked, slide it out of the pan onto a baking tray. Place in the oven to keep warm while you make the remaining five rotis in the same way. Layer sheets of baking parchment between them as you go to prevent them sticking together.

+ Serve at once.

Tasty treats

'Anything is good if it's made of chocolate.'
Jo Brand

I had all sorts of recipe bits and bobs that I wasn't
quite sure where to put – those tasty little things such
as tarts and muffins and easy traybakes that form so
much of my weekend cooking. As my friends and family
can attest, I am often in the kitchen with a whole load
of ingredients, throwing stuff together in a bid to conjure
up some magical, tasty spell. During these times, my
hair is usually grey from icing sugar and there is a
smudge of white chocolate on my chin, but I am always
sporting my gapped-tooth grin with various sweet treats
and other tasty morsels balancing on trays and plates
around my kitchen, many of which can be found here.

Prep time: **15 minutes**
Time baking in the oven:
20-25 minutes
Makes: **12 tarts**
Equipment: **12-hole muffin tin, rolling pin, 7.5cm round cutter, 5cm star cutter, mug or small bowl, pastry brush, wire rack**

A little sunflower oil (or spray oil), for greasing

A handful of plain flour

500g pack of sweet shortcrust pastry (or you can make my sweet rich brown sugar pastry on page 268)

12 tbsp of either one type or a selection of preserves, such as lemon curd, blackberry, strawberry or raspberry jam

1 medium egg

Little jammy tarts

Cutting culinary corners is a huge blessing for me at times and pastry is often not the easiest of things to make. In actual fact, I often encourage people who are starting out with cooking to experiment initially with shop-bought pastry as a way of getting used to it before embarking on making their own. These little jammy tarts evoke happy memories from my youth and eating them whilst still warm from the oven offers me comfort, warmth and calm.

+ Preheat the oven to 180°C, (fan 160°C), 350°F, Gas Mark 4. Lightly grease the muffin tin with oil (an oil spray is handy for this) and set aside.

+ Using a rolling pin, roll the pastry out on a lightly floured work surface to about 5mm thick. Then, using the round cutter and the star cutter, stamp out 12 of each shape. Reroll the pastry as necessary to use it all up.

+ Line each hole of the muffin tin with a pastry disc, very gently pushing them down. Prick a few holes in the bottom of the pastry with a fork, so that it does not puff up when baking. Then spoon a tablespoon of your choice of preserve into each one before sitting a pastry star on top.

+ Crack the egg into a mug or small bowl, whisk lightly with a fork and then brush each star with the egg.

+ Place in the freezer for 5 minutes to harden up a bit so that the butter does not melt before the flour has had a chance to harden (which would leave the tarts in a soggy mess. Anyway, that is not going to happen here.)

+ Remove from the freezer and bake for 20–25 minutes.

+ Once cooked, the pastry should be crisp and golden brown. Leave to cool in the tin for a few minutes before carefully removing onto a wire rack to cool down completely. Now, these are delicious eaten slightly warm, but be careful not to burn yourself with potentially piping hot jam.

Peanut butter squares

Prep time: **25 minutes**
Chilling time: **30 minutes in the freezer (or 1 hour in the fridge)**
Makes: **16 squares**
Equipment: **20cm-square cake tin, large pan, small bowl and microwave or small pan, blender or food processor**

150g butter

200g dark chocolate (minimum 70% cocoa solids) or milk chocolate, or a mixture of both

250g digestive biscuits

200g soft light brown sugar

300g crunchy peanut butter

1 tsp vanilla extract

I was recipe-testing some millionaire's shortbread and found I did not have enough of the correct ingredients. A family-sized pot of crunchy peanut butter sat almost full at the back of my cupboard, providing me with some nutty inspiration for these peanut butter squares.

+ Line the tin with baking parchment, leaving some excess paper hanging over the edges (this makes it easier to lift out once set).

+ Put the butter in a large pan and leave to melt slowly on a low heat.

+ Snap the chocolate into squares and throw into a small bowl. Then melt in the microwave in 30-second blasts, stirring well between each addition. Alternatively, sit the bowl over a pan of simmering water. Make sure that the bottom of the pan does not touch the water or the chocolate may 'seize' and go really grainy and stiff.

+ Remove the butter from the heat once melted.

+ Blitz the digestive biscuits and brown sugar in a blender or food processor to give fine crumbs. Tip them into the butter, scoop in the peanut butter and vanilla extract and mix together well so everything is combined.

+ Tip the mixture into the lined tin and press it down really hard with the back of the spoon. It needs to be really compact and tight. Then pour over the melted chocolate, tilting the tin back and forth a bit so that the whole thing is evenly covered. Pop in the freezer for 30 minutes to firm up (or the fridge for 1 hour).

+ Once the chocolate is set, remove it from the freezer (or fridge). Lift it out of the tin with the help of the baking parchment. Remove the paper and then use a sharp knife to divide it into 16 squares to serve. These will last for a few days in an airtight container.

Prep time: **15 minutes**
Chilling time: **15 minutes in the freezer (or 30 minutes in the fridge)**
Time baking in the oven: **25 minutes**
Cooling time: **about 25 minutes**
Makes: **8 wedges**
Equipment: **Medium bowl, 20cm loose-bottomed round sandwich tin, wire rack**

190g soft butter

120g soft light brown sugar

½ vanilla pod (or a few drops of vanilla extract)

50g roasted chopped hazelnuts (they come ready roasted and chopped from most supermarkets)

280g plain flour

1 egg yolk

Caster sugar, for dusting

Vanilla hazelnut & brown sugar shortbread

The inclusion of soft light brown sugar in this recipe in place of the more common white sugar adds a warm, caramelised taste to the shortbread and deepens its flavour. Hazelnuts add a nutty note, but these can be replaced by any toasted nut of your choice. Try chopping up a little stem ginger and adding that to the mix for a spicy variation too.

+ Put the butter into a medium bowl with the soft light brown sugar and beat together to combine.

+ Split the vanilla pod, scrape out the seeds and add them (or the vanilla extract) to the mixture along with the hazelnuts, flour and egg yolk and mix everything together well. It is kind of a crumbly mixture, so I find the best way to mix it together is to squash everything on the side of the bowl with the back of a wooden spoon to bring it together.

+ Tip the mixture into the sandwich tin. Then I like to get my hands in and squish it all out into a nice flat layer, finishing it off with the back of a spoon to get it really smooth.

+ Now decorate around the edge of the shortbread. Nothing fancy needed here; I just put a little flour on the tips of my index and middle fingers and press them down all the way round the edge of the shortbread to give a nice 'crimped' pattern. Use a knife to lightly mark out eight wedges and use a fork to prick each one three times, to give the shortbread the trademark look.

+ Put this in the freezer for 15 minutes to firm up (or the fridge for 30 minutes). Preheat the oven to 180°C, (fan 160°C), 350°F, Gas Mark 4.

+ Once ready, bake the shortbread for 25 minutes.

+ The shortbread should be just firm and a very light golden colour. Once cooked, remove from the oven and dust with the caster sugar. Allow it to cool in the tin for a few minutes before carefully removing and leaving to cool completely on a wire rack. Then cut it into wedges along the marked-out lines and enjoy. These will keep for a few days in an airtight container.

Blueberry & oat muffins

Prep time. **15 minutes**
Time baking in the oven:
25–30 minutes
Makes: **12 muffins**
Equipment: **Small pan, 12-hole muffin tin, muffin cases (or baking parchment and scissors), large bowl**

100g butter

300g self-raising flour

275g soft light brown sugar (caster sugar will also work)

75g rolled oats

1 tsp baking powder

1 tsp bicarbonate of soda

Pinch of salt

200g fresh or frozen blueberries

300g sour cream

2 medium eggs

1 medium egg yolk

These are my daughter's absolute favourite. I make a huge batch on a Sunday night and she takes them to school to eat at break time. I use sour cream in the recipe, which gives the finished product a wonderful light texture compared to using milk. The trick to a light and fluffy muffin is not to stir the batter too much, but either way they will still taste good.

+ Preheat the oven to 180°C, (fan 160°C), 350°F, Gas Mark 4, with the middle shelf at the ready.

+ Put the butter into a small pan over a low heat and leave to melt.

+ Line the muffin tin with muffin cases or cut out 24 x 15cm squares from the baking parchment. Take two squares and place one on top of the other like a star, then push them down into the muffin tin holes and repeat until all the holes are lined. They may pop up a bit but once the mixture is in, they will stay down!

+ Remove the butter from the heat and leave to cool.

+ Put the flour, sugar, 50g of the oats, the baking powder, bicarbonate of soda and salt into a large bowl, mix together and then make a hole in the centre.

+ Tip two-thirds of the blueberries into the hole, dollop in the sour cream, add the eggs and egg yolk, pour in the cooled melted butter and stir everything gently to just combine. Divide the mixture between the 12 cases. The mixture will give just enough to fill right to the top.

+ Press the remaining blueberries lightly into the tops and then sprinkle the remaining oats evenly over to stick.

+ Bake in the oven for 25–30 minutes or until a skewer inserted into the centre of the muffins comes out clean (try not to hit any blueberries or the skewer will not come out clean). The muffins should also be springy to the touch and golden brown.

+ Eat warm or cold. These will keep for a few days in an airtight container or they freeze well also.

Prep time: 10 minutes
Time baking in the oven:
15 minutes
Makes: 1.3kg
Equipment: 2 large roasting
trays, large bowl

125ml maple syrup

25g caster sugar

25ml sunflower oil

½ tsp vanilla extract

500g jumbo rolled oats

175g mixed seeds (such as pumpkin,
sunflower, sesame or linseeds)

150g pecans (or walnuts)

50g whole almonds

25g flaked almonds

75g desiccated coconut

Pinch of salt (optional)

2 tsp ground cinnamon (optional)

150g dried cranberries

Maple, pecan & cranberry granola

Nutty, fruity, wholesome goodness — a must for the oat lover's kitchen repertoire. Please feel free to ad lib here, with substitutions such as honey for the maple syrup, raisins, apricots or dried apples for the dried cranberries and cashews for the whole almonds.

+ Preheat the oven to 170°C, (fan 150°C), 325°F, Gas Mark 3. Line two large roasting trays with baking parchment and set aside.

+ Put the maple syrup, sugar, oil and vanilla extract into a large bowl and mix well. Then toss in the oats, mixed seeds, pecans (or walnuts), whole almonds, flaked almonds, coconut and salt and cinnamon, if using. Give the mixture a good stir and then get your hands in, picking it up and letting it fall down to coat and moisten everything really well.

+ Pour the mixture onto the roasting trays and spread it out evenly. Bake in the oven for about 15 minutes, giving it a good stir and swapping the trays about on their shelves halfway through.

+ The granola should be golden when cooked. Remove and leave to cool completely before stirring the cranberries through. Store in an airtight container for up to a month.

Port-preserved cherries with cinnamon & orange

Time from start to finish:
**15 minutes
(+ overnight preserving)**
Makes: **about 900g or fills a
725ml jar**
Equipment: **Small saucepan,
725ml Kilner or jam jar (with lid),
zester, colander**

300g soft light brown sugar

150ml port

1 tsp ground cinnamon

1 orange

150ml water

350g fresh cherries

These are delicious nibbled on straight from the jar or served warm or at room temperature with anything chocolatey or creamy. The stones are still in the cherries, so it might be best to warn people of this first!

+ Sterilise a Kilner or jam jar (and its lid) in the dishwasher on the hottest wash or carefully put them in just-boiled water (off the heat) for a couple of minutes and dry with a clean towel.

+ Put the sugar, port and cinnamon in a small saucepan and finely grate the orange zest in. Halve and juice the orange, adding the juice with 150ml of water.

+ Then bring everything slowly to the boil, stirring every so often until the sugar dissolves. Let it boil away for 3 minutes until thick and syrupy and then remove and leave to cool.

+ Meanwhile, wash the cherries in a colander and remove their stalks if wished, but I think they look great left on. Place them in the sterilised jar.

+ Once cooled, pour the syrup over the cherries and leave to sit at least overnight. The cherries will last for a week if kept nice and airtight in the jar.

Prep time: **15 minutes**
Chilling time: **15 minutes**
Makes: **about 40**
Equipment: **Large tray or baking sheet, medium bowl and microwave or medium pan, colander**

100g white chocolate

500g cherries (preferably with stalks still attached)

White chocolate-dipped cherries

I was driving around northern Spain last year and was taken aback by the many, many cherries for sale by the roadside. Big fat cherries bursting with juice and as shiny as a mirror. But after my third bag, I felt they needed a bit of variation. Having found a jumbo bar of white chocolate in the fridge, this 'recipe' was born. If you fancy it, after dipping the cherries in the white chocolate, dip them in some blitzed-up nuts for a bit of variation.

+ Line a large tray or baking sheet with baking parchment and then set this aside.

+ Break the chocolate into a medium bowl. I like to melt chocolate in a microwave in 30-second blasts, stirring between each blast. Alternatively, melt the chocolate in a bowl that just sits on top of a medium pan with a little bit of boiling water. Just make sure the bowl doesn't touch the water as this could make the chocolate grainy.

+ White chocolate is more difficult to melt than dark or milk. There is a fine line between it being just melted and it burning and drying out (where it becomes thick and 'doughy'). Keep a close eye on it and as soon as it starts melting, stir for a few seconds and then remove from the heat.

+ Wash the cherries in a colander and pat dry with kitchen paper. Then, holding a cherry by the stalk, dip it halfway into the melted chocolate. I like to dip them at a slight angle as I think it looks a bit cooler. Then shake off the excess and sit the cherry, stalk side up on the tray or baking sheet. Repeat with the rest of the cherries.

+ Place the coated cherries in the fridge for at least 15 minutes, or until the chocolate hardens, before serving. I think these look so pretty when presented all together on a big plate or cake stand.

Prep time: 10 minutes for disc
lollipops or 20 minutes for trellis-
type
Chilling time: 15 minutes
Makes: about 10 lollipops
Equipment: Large tray or baking
sheet, 10 cocktail or lollipop
sticks, medium bowl and medium
pan or microwave, scissors and
sticky tape or stapler (optional)

100g white chocolate
1 tbsp dried cranberries

White chocolate lollipops with dried cranberries

The best chocolate for these lollipops is cheap white children's chocolate. You can use sprinkles, nuts or other dried fruits for these; just about anything that does not have too much of a water content will work.

+ Line a large tray or baking sheet with baking parchment so the paper is really flat (making sure that the tray will fit in the fridge a bit later on). Lay the cocktail or lollipop sticks out on the sheet, spaced well apart.

+ Snap the chocolate up a bit into a medium bowl and either melt in the microwave in 30-second blasts, stirring between each addition, or set over a pan of simmering water, making sure that the bottom of the bowl does not touch the water.

+ White chocolate is more difficult to melt than dark or milk. There is a fine line between it being just melted and it burning and drying out (where it becomes thick and 'doughy'). Keep a close eye on it and as soon as it starts melting, stir for a few seconds and then remove from the heat.

+ If making disc lollipops, simply place a spoonful of melted chocolate on top of one end of each of the sticks to give a 4cm disc. If making trellis type lollipops, cut out a 12.5cm square of baking parchment, then roll it into a cone shape and gently pull the flap on the inside to tighten the whole thing and create a nozzle tip. Secure down the side with some sticky tape or a stapler, then snip the tip with scissors to give a 5mm nozzle opening. Spoon the melted chocolate in and fold down the top of the piping bag so the chocolate does not squidge out the wrong end.

+ Gently squeeze the chocolate from the piping bag to draw whatever shape you like over one end of each of the sticks. Flick it over and back in a crisscross pattern or go around and around in circles, for example.

+ Once your chosen lollipop shapes have been made, finely chop the cranberries and scatter them over the chocolate to stick.

+ Place them in the fridge for at least 15 minutes or until set. Very carefully peel the lollipops off the paper and serve. They will keep for up to a month in the fridge (if they have survived being eaten!).

Prep time: 10 minutes
Chilling time: 25 minutes in the freezer or 50 minutes in the fridge
Coating time: 10–15 minutes (depending on which finish you go for)
Makes: 18–20 lollipops
Equipment: Large baking tray, food processor (or plastic food bag, rolling pin and medium bowl), 18–20 x 15cm (approx) lollipop sticks (the white rounded type), small bowl and microwave or small pan, small bowls

Lollipops

2 x 154g packs of Oreo cookies

150g cream cheese (or chocolate cream cheese or Nutella)

Coating

200g white chocolate (the cheapest you can find)

2 tsp (per lollipop) of hundreds and thousands or chopped nuts (optional)

Shameless shortcut cookies-and-cream lollipops

White chocolate is a curious beast as it is not really chocolate, containing no actual cocoa solids whatsoever. Because of this, it tends to go lumpy and thick more quickly than our darker chocolate friends. So if you find when using it that it becomes gloopy, just melt it again and it should come good. The lollipops can be dipped in hundreds and thousands or chopped nuts after being dipped in the white chocolate if you fancy it.

+ Line a large baking tray (that will fit in your freezer or fridge) with baking parchment and set aside.

+ Tip the Oreos into a food processor and whiz them up to fine crumbs. Then add the cream cheese (or chocolate cream cheese or Nutella) and whiz until the mixture starts to form a ball.

+ If you are not using a food processor, pop the cookies in a plastic food bag and bash them to fine crumbs with a rolling pin. Tip them into a medium bowl and stir in the cream cheese (or chocolate cream cheese or Nutella) until the mixture begins to stick together.

+ With cold hands, roll the mixture into 18–20 equal-sized balls, about 3cm in diameter. The size doesn't matter too much, it's just a guideline, but make sure you squidge them together really firmly so that they stay together. Place them on the prepared tray as you go and then put them in the freezer for 15 minutes, or the fridge for 30 minutes, to firm up.

+ Once they are ready, melt the chocolate in a microwave in 30-second blasts, stirring between each blast, or in a small bowl over a pan of simmering water, making sure that the bottom of the bowl does not touch the water otherwise the chocolate may go all grainy and hard.

>

Shameless shortcut
cookies-and-cream
lollipops

(continued)

+ Remove the balls from the fridge/freezer. Dip the end of a lollipop stick into the melted chocolate and then push that end into a ball so it goes in about 1–2cm. Repeat with the rest of the balls, laying them back on the tray as you go.

+ Dip the balls into the remaining chocolate one at a time, swirling them about a bit and then leaving the excess to drip back into the bowl. Stand them up on the tray (so with the sticks pointing upright).

+ If using a coating like the hundreds and thousands or chopped nuts, then have them ready in small bowls before you coat the balls in chocolate. Then once the balls are covered, dip them straight into the coating of choice until completely or even just half covered, whatever you fancy.

+ Return them to the freezer for 10 minutes (or the fridge for about 20 minutes) until set. If they are going into the freezer, they may need to be put lying down, which is completely fine.

+ To serve, either stand them on a platter or cake stand (as they are on the tray) or put them upright in a glass so the balls are on top.

Time from start to finish:
15 minutes
Makes: **500ml**
Equipment: **Medium pan,
large bowl**

500ml whole milk

1 vanilla pod (or a few drops of
vanilla extract)

6 medium egg yolks

100g caster sugar

Homemade vanilla custard (crème anglaise)

This custard recipe is also great for making ice cream, so if you have an ice-cream maker, you can churn it to make beautifully silky vanilla ice cream.

+ Pour the milk into a medium pan on a low to medium heat. Halve the vanilla pod, scrape the seeds out and add them also (you can chuck the pod in too, unless you prefer to add it to your sugar pot to make vanilla sugar) or add the vanilla extract, if using. Leave to come slowly to the boil.

+ Meanwhile, put the egg yolks and sugar into a large bowl and mix them together gently.

+ As soon as the milk is boiling, remove it from the heat and carefully fish the vanilla pod out (if it was used). Keep the pan close by as you will need it again.

+ Sit the egg mixture bowl on a tea towel to stop it from spinning around and then, stirring all the time, slowly pour the milk into the egg mixture. Continue to mix it together for about 20 seconds and then pour everything back into the milk pan.

+ Return the pan to a very low heat and cook the custard very gently for 7–8 minutes, stirring all the time. It's important to stay with it as it could turn to scrambled eggs easily.

+ To test when it is ready, lift the wooden spoon out of the mixture. The custard should coat the back of the spoon nicely. It won't be really thick like our shop-bought friend, but it will be a little thicker than double cream. If you want to make it thicker, put some cornflour into a mug, add a little of the custard and then tip the whole lot back into the pan. Cook for a minute or so and then pour through a sieve (to get rid of any lumps). Pour the finished custard into a serving jug and serve hot.

Time from start to finish:
20 minutes, plus a further
10 minutes if preparing your
own mangoes
Makes: 1 litre
Equipment: Large pan, zester,
blender or food processor, Kilner
or jam jars (and their lids) with a
total capacity of 1 litre

3 x 250g packs of ready-prepared
mango cubes or 5 medium–large ripe
mangoes

150ml sherry or apple cider vinegar

300g granulated sugar

2 cloves

2 star anise

1 cinnamon stick

1 bunch of spring onions

2 garlic cloves

3 red chillies

2cm piece of fresh ginger

1 orange

Salt and freshly ground black pepper

Mango chutney

To prepare containers for the chutney, sterilise the Kilner or jam jars (and their lids). I like to do this in the dishwasher on the hottest wash, or you could carefully put them in just-boiled water (off the heat) for a couple of minutes and dry with a clean towel.

+ If using whole mangoes, prepare them first (if using prepared packs, then skip happily onto the next step). Slice the two cheeks off either side of the stone. Cut them in half and then run the knife through the flesh close to the skin to peel it. Dice the flesh into bite-sized pieces and scatter on a big serving platter. I like to slice off the remaining skinny sides of mango and use them so as not to waste any.

+ For the chutney, pour the vinegar and sugar into a large pan and add the cloves, star anise and cinnamon stick. Bring slowly to the boil, stirring until the sugar dissolves.

+ Meanwhile, trim and finely slice the spring onions (the green and white bits) and peel and finely chop the garlic and set aside.

+ Once boiling, whack the heat up under the pan and leave the vinegar mixture to boil hard for 3 minutes until thickened and syrupy.

+ Meanwhile, deseed and finely chop the red chillies, peel and finely chop the ginger and finely grate the zest of the orange.

+ Stir the spring onions, garlic, chillies, ginger and orange zest into the syrup along with the mango pieces. Cook on a rolling boil for 8 minutes.

+ Once the mango is soft, remove from the heat and leave to cool for a moment. Then ladle about half of the mixture into a blender or processor and pulse a few times to give a fairly smooth pulp. Stir this back into the rest of the mixture and season with salt and pepper to taste. Then ladle it into sterilised jars.

+ Leave to cool completely in a cool place with a piece of kitchen paper over the top, so that it can breathe but no dust or anything can get in it. Then, once cool, pop the lids on and store in a cool dry place for a couple of weeks or in the fridge for up to 1 month. You now have some really tasty mango and orange chutney!

Homemade vanilla extract

Prep time: **15 minutes, plus at least 24 hours to infuse**
Makes: **200ml**
Equipment: **250ml Kilner or jam jar (with lid), small pan**

50ml dark or white rum
150g granulated sugar
100ml water
4 vanilla pods

Buying vanilla pods in the shops is not the most pleasant experience as they do not come cheap. However, slam 'vanilla pods' into any search engine and places will come up that sell them wholesale. Most people don't want to buy a whole wad of these pods, but they do sell them in 'domestic' quantities. What friends of mine have done is to group together and place an order at the same time. Once you have scraped the seeds from the pod to use in another recipe, pop the vanilla stick into your jar of sugar syrup. If you are an avid baker, before too long you will have lots of sticks in your jar with the residual seeds left in them, making the most delicious vanilla extract you can imagine. If, however, you are impatient and keen to get going, then just follow the recipe below, buying four vanilla pods and sticking them in a jar so you can use your vanilla extract straight away. Great to decant into little bottles (again, you can find them online), then just cut the vanilla pods in half, and give them away as presents as part of a homemade hamper.

+ Sterilise a Kilner or jam jar (and its lid) in the dishwasher on the hottest wash or carefully put them in just-boiled water (off the heat) for a couple of minutes and dry with a clean towel.

+ Put the rum and sugar in a small pan with 100ml of water. Set on a low to medium heat and stir from time to time until the sugar has dissolved. Then whack up the heat and bring it to the boil. Once boiling, leave it to bubble away for 5 minutes and then take it off the heat to cool a little.

+ Pour the cooled sugar syrup into the sterilised jar. Split the vanilla pods all the way down their length, add them to the syrup and leave to cool completely. Then put the lid on and leave for at least 24 hours to infuse.

Acknowledgements

Acknowledgements are always such a hard thing to write. There is a constant fear that I am going to leave someone out who has been instrumental in getting me to where I am today. So I will start by saying if I do indeed forget anyone, then please do forgive me. It has been a busy year to say the least, with all sorts of highs and lows but through it all there has been a group of people who have kept me going through the thick of it.

Firstly, I would like to say the most sincerest of thank yous to the incredible team at James Grant: Nicola Ibison, Mary Bekhait, Neil Rodford, Darren Worsley, Paul Worsley, Sunil Singhvi, Riz Mansor, Charlotte Hanbury, who came to my rescue at a time when I was lying in a proverbial heap on the floor and carried me to safety. The way the whole team has been there for me goes far beyond the reaches of just being managers and for that I will always, always be forever grateful.

Lisa Edwards, Alison Kirkham, Janice Hadlow, Rebecca Ford, Emma Swain and Nick Patten, who have been absolute rocks for me at the BBC. Thank you for believing in me and giving me this incredible platform to do what I so, so love to do: talk about food.

Pete Lawrence, Amy Joyce, Ceri Turnbull, Martin Morrison (Edit Producer/ setting up inserts), Sophie Wells (Assistant Producer), Claire Martin (Assistant Producer), Angela Hall (Production Manager), Gina Waggott, Simon Weekes, Sam Key, Jamie Dobbs, Bill Rudolph, Paul Allen, Ben Sanderson, Neusa Love, Rupert Trotski (Editor) and Gary Thomas, Rudi Thackeray and Helen Mooney, the set design team. And the brilliant director, Ben Warwick.

The very brilliant and super-fast Michaela Bowles and her efficient and ever-smiling team: Phil Wells, Katy Ross (who were both in most days), Stella Murphy, Chrissie Chung and Sammy Jo Squire.

The very precise and efficient Sharon Hearne-Smith for checking my recipes so very thoroughly.

And of course the stellar book team at HarperCollins: Victoria Barnsley, Belinda Budge, Barnaby Dawe and Carole Tonkinson, who is at the helm of my team. Thank you, Carole, for your razor sharp instinct, your attention to detail and your constant support. Additionally Georgina Atsiaris, Martin Topping, Katrina O'Neill and Monica Green back at Hammersmith HQ. Thanks to Katie Giovanni and Julia Azzarello for the food styling of the book and Lisa Harrison for the props. Thanks also to Diana Colbert.

Myles New… your photos are ace…

Carlos Ferraz, the pics in the book are divine – thank you for de-worzel-gummidging my hair and making it look lovely.

My love will always go out to the team at Storm Management.

Thanks also to Simon Fuller and the XIX team.

Huge hugs and love go out to all the members of my family who have been there since those early days of me arriving to the fold with a penchant for three Shredded Wheat (with no milk). Mum, Dad, Jace, Kate, Fran, Rachel, Auntie Angela, Victoria, James and my inspiring daughter Ella. And, of course, my awesome partner and my best friend, Ged.

Rodney, Tony Walker, Velm, Benjamin Christopherson, Judy Joo, Lia Peralta, Ewan Venters, Maggie Draycot, Norie Lagmay, Keith Stoll, Satya and all my friends who have been there for me… at all hours.

Jonathan Lomax and the team at Lomax, thank you for keeping me trim.

Thanks to all my facebook and twitter followers!

Big shout out to TACT Care, Rays of Sunshine, The Prince's Trust, Barnado's and Sutton Community Farm. I hope I can help you more in 2013.

Thank you!

Lorraine

*'Dripping water hollows out a stone not through force
but by persistance.'*
Ovid

Index

five-spice roasted duck breasts with cherry &
    Shiraz sauce 119
French onion & sage soup with croutons 65
fritters: Aussie sweetcorn breakfast fritters 45

G

garlic
    bread, warm 63
    potato wedges 124
gazpacho: red pepper, tomato & basil
    gazpacho 60
ginger
    butternut squash 167
    lemon dressing 153
    mascarpone cream 233
    sesame & ginger noodles 193
    stem ginger whipped cream 222
    zesty apple sauce with cinnamon &
        ginger 295
gingerbread pancakes with Parma ham &
    maple syrup 51
gnocchi: pan-fried mascarpone gnocchi with
    dreamy basil pesto 212
goat's cheese
    goat's cheese, figs & mint with balsamic
        drizzle 12
    goat's cheese, toasted hazelnut & honey
        quesadillas 198
    on pizza 42
good old-fashioned burger with rocket, red
    onions & garlicky potato wedges 124
granola: maple, pecan & cranberry granola
    280
Greek spinach, feta & pine nut pie with dill &
    crunchy filo 205
guacamole 23

H

harissa
    chicken cacciatore with harissa, bacon &
        rosemary 113
    hummus 20
    on pizza 42
hazelnut, vanilla & brown sugar shortbread
    276
herby dumplings 127
homemade vanilla custard (crème anglaise)
    292
homemade vanilla extract 296
honey
    goat's cheese, toasted hazelnut & honey
        quesadillas 198
    honey & mustard dip 15
    honey soy-glazed salmon with sesame &
        ginger noodles 193
horseradish crème fraîche 84
hot-smoked trout kedgeree with spring onions
    & basil 180

hot-and-sour king prawn soup 59
hummus
    hummus with cumin & paprika 24
    on pizza 42
    harissa 20

J

jam
    little jammy tarts 272
    sweet chilli 45
jello shots
    lemoncello 27
    watermelon 28

K

kale & basil pesto 190
kedgeree: hot-smoked trout kedgeree with
    spring onions & basil 180

L

lamb
    Lozza's lamb biryani 142
    maple and balsamic-glazed lamb chops
        with mint 139
    mighty moussaka 136
    rosemary roast cottage pie with a crispy
        rosti topping 130
    slow-roast, fast-prep leg of lamb with
        Aussie Chardonnay, rosemary, sage
        & bay 145
lasagne: butternut & sweet potato lasagne
    201
leek: potato & leek vichyssoise with crispy
    bacon & chives 55
lemon
    lemon & ginger dressing 153
    lemon & lime poppy seed drizzle cake
        247
    lemoncello jello shots 27
    lovely limoncello 35
lemoncello jello shots 27
lentils: warm salmon & lentils 184
let them eat cake, cake 248
lime
    coriander crème fraîche 207
    lemon & lime poppy seed drizzle cake
        247
little jammy tarts 272
little warm Bramley apple pies or 'chaussons
    aux pommes' 216
lollipops
    shameless shortcut cookies-and-cream
        lollipops 288
    white chocolate lollipops with dried
        cranberries 287
lovely limoncello 35
Lozza's lamb biryani 142

M

mackerel salad with horseradish crème
    fraîche 84
mango
    chutney 293
    mango, feta & avocado salad 70
    salsa 107
    Union cobb 88
maple syrup
    gingerbread pancakes with Parma ham &
        maple syrup 51
    maple, pecan & cranberry granola 280
    maple syrup and balsamic-glazed lamb
        chops with mint, toasted almonds and
        feta cous cous 139
mascarpone
    broccoli & blue cheese soup with chive
        mascarpone 63
    pan-fried mascarpone gnocchi 212
    pear, almond & amaretto tart.with stem
        ginger mascarpone cream 233
meringues 225
    blackberry Eton mess 222
mighty moussaka 136
mojitos, strawberry & mint 32
Moroccan pesto fish with caramelised onions
    & haricot beans served with minty pine
    nut cous cous 169
mousse: chocolate with raspberries 227
muffins, blueberry & oat 279
mushroom
    & mustard sauce, creamy 150
    vegetarian mushroom & port 'faux gras'
        with tarragon & chestnuts 38
mustard
    Gruyère & mustard croutons 65
    honey mustard dip 15
    & mushroom sauce, creamy 150

N

naughty, naughty nachos 23
neat-and-tidy Eton mess with blackberries &
    stem ginger whipped cream 222
net bread (roti jala) 265
nifty Niçoise salad with hot-smoked trout &
    sundried tomatoes 87
noodles
    red pepper 179
    sesame 119
    sesame & ginger 193

O

oats
    blueberry & oat muffins 279
    maple, pecan & cranberry granola 280
olives: Aussie olive damper bread 256
onion
    caramelised, with beans 169